# THE SAVOUR OF SALT
*A Henry Salt Anthology*

# THE SAVOUR OF SALT

## A Henry Salt Anthology

"... I felt flattered by the remark of a hostile journalist that I was 'a compendium of the cranks', by which he apparently meant that I advocated not this or that humane reform, but all of them. That is just what I desire to do."

Henry Salt, *The Creed of Kinship*

Edited by
## GEORGE HENDRICK
and
## WILLENE HENDRICK

CENTAUR PRESS
FONTWELL SUSSEX
1989

First published 1989 by Centaur Press Limited,
Fontwell, Sussex BN18 0TA

British Library Cataloguing in Publication Data

Salt, Henry S. (Henry Stephens) *1851 – 1939*
    The savour of salt : a Henry Salt anthology
    1. Social reform
    I. Title II. Hendrick, George III. Hendrick,
    Willene
    303.4'84

ISBN 0-900001-30-5

Typeset in Palatino by Pauline Newton, Chichester, West Sussex
Printed in Great Britain by Antony Rowe Ltd, Chippenham, Wiltshire

# CONTENTS

CONTENTS

# PREFACE

HENRY SALT (1851–1939) published some forty books, most of them long out of print and highly prized by collectors. Among them was one of the most noteworthy biographies of Henry David Thoreau (the 1896 edition being reprinted in 1968 by Archon Press), as well as important studies of Richard Jefferies, De Quincey, and Percy Bysshe Shelley who had a considerable influence on Salt when he was at Eton.

Following his death in 1939, this interesting radical reformer was forgotten until Stephen Winsten's book *Salt and His Circle* appeared in 1951. Sadly, it had a limited circulation and Salt was again forgotten until the University of Illinois Press published George Hendrick's *Henry Salt: Humanitarian Reformer and Man of Letters* in 1977. Salt's determination to remove social and economic abuses called for the emancipation of men and animals from injustice and cruelty. He campaigned against one of the most disagreeable characteristics of mankind — a general indifference towards Nature. This is fully acknowledged in Salt's literary craftsmanship, integrity and kindness, and clearly revealed by Hendrick.

Victorian *extraordinaire*, vegetarian, ethical socialist, naturalist and follower of Thoreau, he traversed his beloved Lake District and the mountains of Wales and Scotland, promoting his flow of thoughts about man's relation with Nature. Long before conservation was being seriously considered he expressed with deep passion his concerns about chemical waste in lakes and streams, the despoiling of mountains, and the destruction of 'wild places'. He appealed for the establishment of National Parks and for the protection of wildflowers and wild-life in 'sanctuaries'.

Salt's philosophy was based upon the principle that "it is iniquitous to inflict unnecessary suffering on any sentient being".

7

He attacked the brutality of flogging in the Royal Navy, the ill-treatment of the poor in hospitals, the penal system, the barbaric practices of master and workman towards domestic animals, and vivisection. He was secretary for nearly thirty years of The Humanitarian League, and with much good humour was ready to do battle against the prejudices of individual and institution alike. Support came mainly from his many literary friends — Edward Carpenter, G.W. Foote, Thomas Hardy, W.H. Hudson, W.M. Hyndman, George Meredith, William Morris, Lord (Sidney) Olivier, and Bernard Shaw.

Salt's *Animals' Rights Considered in Relation to Social Progress* was first published in 1892. It was reprinted in 1980 by the Pennsylvania-based Society for Animal Rights and by the Centaur Press in England. This seminal monograph anticipated the present on-going debate about changing individual and institutional attitudes towards "our fellow creatures". Salt thoroughly examined the subject, drawing examples from modern and classical literatures and from his serious study of Victorian and Edwardian Britain. Many of his observations are still relevant to-day. It is interesting to note that special editions were printed in Europe and that through the generosity of a Miss Eddy of Providence, Rhode Island, *Animals' Rights* was distributed free to libraries in the United States.

Salt's obituaries in the London press, especially *The Times* and the *Daily Telegraph*, recognized the unique qualities of this classical scholar who had given up 'The Good Life' for 'The Simple Life', which he found more congenial and in keeping with his views. His deep sympathy for all sentient beings and his faith in 'Brotherhood' determined his last book, *A Creed of Kinship*, published four years before his death. Salt was soon forgotten and neglected by the Socialist movement which he had so long served. His ethical embrace of many causes was too much for the doctrinaire influences of the Fabians.

*The Savour of Salt* must prompt a new appraisal of a man whose deep and applied humanity was marked by a rare humour and a notable mastery of words. In his simple and dedicated life he exemplified the central message to be found in this book, echoing the words of Lao Tse: "The way to do is to be."

JOHN F. PONTIN

# INTRODUCTION

THIS VOLUME pays tribute to Henry Stephens Shakespear Salt, that child of privilege who became a partisan of ethical socialism and a tireless worker for humanitarian reform. When he died in Brighton, England, in 1939 he had prepared his own funeral address, which was read by his friend Bertram Lloyd. In that statement Salt touched on the many concerns of his mature life: "... [W]hen I say that I shall die, as I have lived, a rationalist, socialist, pacifist and humanitarian, I must make my meaning clear. I wholly disbelieve in the present established religion; but I have a very firm religious faith of my own — a Creed of Kinship, I call it — a belief that in years yet to come there will be a recognition of the brotherhood between man and man, nation and nation, human and sub-human, which will transform a state of semi-savagery, as we have it, into one of civilization, when there will be no such barbarity as warfare, or the robbery of the poor by the rich, or the ill-usage of the lower animals by mankind."

Who was this man with views most people in his (and our) generation found (and find) puzzling, or perverse, or revolutionary, or eccentric, or naive, or merely overly idealistic? Salt was born in India in 1851, the son of Colonel T.H. Salt of the Royal Bengal Artillery. Colonel and Mrs Salt were not happily married, and when Henry was one, he and his mother returned to England, where much of his childhood was spent in the Shrewsbury home of his maternal grandparents, the Allnatts. He grew up in a well-to-do family which traced its lineage back to King Frederick I of Denmark. He was coached for Eton by the Reverend C. Kegan Paul, the radical minister who was later a prominent London publisher. Salt then attended Eton as a King's Scholar, and some of the happiest years of his life were spent there.

He seems to have been an excellent student. He also made many friends, and this was a characteristic of Salt throughout his life. Even though he became a religious and social and political radical, and his classmates did not, he could, fifty years after leaving Eton, meet an old schoolfellow and they could resume their "acquaintance on the former footing as easily as if we had been next door neighbours all the time."

From Eton Salt went to Cambridge, but he was unhappy there, even though he had a brilliant academic career. He found that there was almost no concern at that ancient university for "the higher social ethics". He received a call to return to Eton as an assistant master, which offered the prospect of a comfortable life. But although "new ideas" seldom penetrated that respectable institution, the social, religious, and political ferment of the time did not escape his attention and concern. His conversion from respectability to radicalism took several years, and during that time of change he married Catherine Leigh Joynes, daughter of the Lower Master at Eton. Bernard Shaw, a close friend of the Salts, insisted that the tragedy of Salt's life was that Kate Salt would not consummate the marriage and had lesbian affairs. Salt himself never touched on this subject in his published writings, but this unconventional marriage must have played some role in his changing intellectual and social views. He met Shaw, Edward Carpenter, William Morris, John Ruskin and other socialists and radical thinkers and began to explore the various socialist organizations in Victorian England. He was also converted to vegetarianism, in many ways more heretical than socialism "because it had to be practised as well as preached, and the abstinence from flesh-foods could not fail to attract unfavourable attention". He read Thoreau's *Walden* at this critical period of his life and determined to follow the example of the Concord philosopher and live more simply and more independently.

In time Salt realized that he could stay at Eton no longer, for he had come to believe that the masters were cannibals, living off animal flesh and exploiting working class people who did the "hard work of the world". When Salt visited the headmaster to make his farewells, Dr Warre "expressed his regret that I had lost faith in that public school system to which he himself, as all Etonians are aware, devoted a lifetime of unsparing service. 'It's the Vegetarianism', he gravely remarked; and I understood him to mean that it was the abandonment of the orthodox diet that had led . . . to my apostasy in regard to Education. When I told him that Socialism must take its share of blame, as having been at least an auxiliary cause, he was really shocked. 'Socialism!' he cried, in his hearty tones. 'Then blow us up, blow us up! There's nothing left for it but that.' ''

In 1885 the Salts began their new life, living without servants, entertaining their new friends, and working for various radical causes. One of their closest friends was Edward Carpenter, a fellow Thoreauvian who shared their own views on Simplification. Salt made many contacts with reformers through Jim Joynes, his brother-in-law, who had also left Eton to work with radical groups. Salt knew the leaders of the socialist organizations: the Social Democratic Federation, the Fellowship of the New Life, and the Fabians. Working in these organizations he met Sidney Olivier, the Webbs, Prince Kropotkin, and many others. He published serious, scholarly essays on the failure of the educational system at Eton and began to publish poems and essays in the socialist newspaper *Justice*. He wrote a mocking attack on the *laissez-faire* economic system in a poem entitled "A Song of Freedom", ending with this biting verse:

> So, hey! for England's glorious rights;
> Free sellin' and free buyin',
> Free libraries; free pews; free fights,
> And a free ditch — to die in!

In addition to his reform work, Salt began writing serious literary criticism on a wide range of English-speaking authors: Lord Tennyson, John Barlas, Francis Adams, Henry Thoreau, Herman Melville, Nathaniel Hawthorne, Percy Bysshe Shelley, James Thomson (B.V.), Thomas De Quincey, and many others. One of his greatest achievements as a biographer and critic was his *Life of Thoreau*, still one of the most perceptive and best-written studies of the Concord naturalist-philosopher. Salt's several studies on Shelley were also outstanding. He recognized Shelley's poetic abilities and praised him for being the "uncompromising champion of the people's rights and true liberty of thought and action . . ." Salt was a gifted biographer and critic whose works have stood the test of time.

By 1891 Salt had developed a world view which embraced

socialism, vegetarianism, pacificism, anti-vivisectionism, and various other "isms". Humanitarianism was the name he adopted for this philosophy, and in 1891 a group of like-minded people joined him to found the Humanitarian League which asserted "that much good will be done by the mere placing on record of a systematic and consistent protest against the numerous barbarisms of civilization — the cruelties inflicted by men on men, in the name of law, authority, and traditional habit, and the still more atrocious ill-treatment of the so-called lower animals, for the purpose of 'sport', 'science', 'fashion', and the gratification of an appetite for unnatural food."

Salt knew that the Humanitarian cause would have little popular support, but the aims of the organization were ably furthered by two journals edited by Salt: *Humanity*, later renamed *The Humanitarian* (1895 – 1919), and *The Humane Review* (1900 – 1910). Salt wrote hundreds of thousands of words for these journals and single-handedly carried on the secretarial and the organizational work of the League. He published the scholarly, well reasoned *Animals' Rights* in 1892, reprinted and revised over the years and translated into several languages. He argued, citing copious examples, that animals, as well as men, should be "exempt from any unnecessary suffering or serfdom". Salt the rationalist and classicist is evident as he contrasted Christian attitudes toward animals with Buddhistic statements on the sacredness of all life and with Seneca, Plutarch, and other classical writers, who "took the still higher ground in preaching humanity on the broadest principle of universal benevolence".

In addition to working for animals' rights and vegetarianism, Salt and the League campaigned for slaughterhouse reform, for prison reform, for conservation of areas of natural beauty, and for peace. Salt wrote a steady stream of essays, books, and poems urging reforms, as well as two one-act plays: *A Lover of Animals* and *The Home Secretary's Holiday*.

The League ended after the barbarism of the First World War, and Salt recognized that the organization was "a Forlorn Hope; that is, a troop of venturesome pioneers, who were quite untrammelled by 'prospects', and whose whim it was to open out a path by which others might eventually follow". The Humanitarian League indeed opened a path which slowly increasing numbers have taken.

Salt's account of the growth of his own ethical concerns for man and animals is to be found in his splendid *Seventy Years Among Savages* (1921), one of the most thoughtful autobiographies of this century. He also wrote an account of his many friendships in *Company I Have Kept* (1930). These friendships included socialists such as Shaw; ethical revolutionaries such as Mahatma Gandhi; literary specialists such as the Thoreauvian Dr Samuel Arthur Jones; and many others. He was a tolerant man, and he consistently, and often with humour, saw beyond personal quirks to the essential nature of people.

After the death of his first wife in 1919 and the disbanding of the Humanitarian League, Salt kept busy with his writing and his nature studies. He married Catherine Mandeville in 1927, and this second marriage was a happy one, bringing tranquillity and contentment to his life.

During his last years Salt wrote *The Call of the Wildflower*, a plea for nature conservation; he completed a translation of Virgil; he wrote his evocative *Memories of Bygone Eton*; he defended his political beliefs in The Heart of Socialism; he published the second volume of his autobiography, *Company I Have Kept*; and he brought together his verses and epigrams in *Cum Grano*. He never turned his back on the humanitarian principles which he had promulgated for many years. Four years before his death he summed up those beliefs in the moving *Creed of Kinship*, which restated all the ethical concerns he had been supporting for years: his plea for animals' rights; his attacks upon the barbarism of cruel sports, vivisection, and flesh eating; his defense of socialism; his call for pacifism; and his belief in the Creed of Kinship which called for "a charter of human and sub-human relationships".

He died in obscurity, but fifty years later, in a time perhaps more barbaric than his own, his ethical concerns are as powerful as when he wrote them. This anthology brings together some of his best writings, illuminating for a new generation of readers Salt's vision of a better world.

WILLENE HENDRICK AND GEORGE HENDRICK

# ACKNOWLEDGMENTS

For permission to reproduce passages from George Hendrick's *Henry Salt: Humanitarian Reformer and Man of Letters*, and Fritz Oehlschlaeger and George Hendrick's *Toward the Making of Thoreau's Modern Reputation*, we are indebted to the University of Illinois Press. The library of the University of Illinois at Urbana-Champaign has given us permission to publish Salt letters in its collections. We wish to express our appreciation to Philip Melancon, John F. Pontin, MaryAnn Violin, and Jon Wynne-Tyson for many favours.

# A NOTE ON THE TEXT

We have included some entire chapters from Salt's works. In a few cases we have omitted words or a sentence or sentences, and in those instances we use ellipses to indicate that omission. A few obvious typographical errors have been silently corrected.

# I
# HENRY SALT: REFORMER

REFORM was in the air in the 1880s when the Salts left Eton, and Salt spent the rest of his long life working for causes. This section begins with Salt's introduction to *Seventy Years Among Savages*, a book which summed up his activities as a reformer. We then include material on the two movements which first attracted his talents: Vegetarianism, a major component of his attempt to simplify his life and to live more ethically, and "Socialism, the more equitable distribution of wealth." After helping organize the Humanitarian League, Salt championed many causes, and we have included chapters from his books and pamphlets which set out his views on animals' rights, his arguments against flogging and other human tortures and for prison reform, and which describe his crusades against "blood sports" and the killing of birds and animals for a frivolous fashion industry. Here is concrete evidence of Salt's passionate embrace of many different causes.

In this section and in those to follow, we will sprinkle a few of Salt's poems and apt prose quotations here and there to season the longer pieces.

EDITORS

## THE ARGUMENT

A strange lot this, to be dropped down in a world of barbarians—Men who
see clearly enough the barbarity of all ages except their own!—ERNEST CROSBY

The tales of travellers, from Herodotus to Marco Polo, and from
Marco Polo to the modern "globe-trotter," have in all ages been
subject, justly or unjustly, to a good deal of suspicion, on the
ground that those who go in quest of curious information among
outlandish tribes are likely in the first instance to be imposed on
themselves, and in the sequel to impose on their readers. No such
doubt, however, can attach to the following record, for I am
myself a native of the land whose customs are described by me.
I cannot think that my story, true as it is, and admitting of
corroboration by the similar witness of others, is any the less
adventurous on that account; for, like previous writers who have
recorded certain startling discoveries, I, too, have to speak of
solitudes and remotenesses, vast deserts and rare oases, inex-
tricable forests and dividing gulfs; and such experiences are none
the less noteworthy because they are not of the body but of the
mind. At any rate, the tale which I have to tell deals with incidents
which have had a very real significance for myself — quite as real
as any of those related by the most venturesome of voyagers.

The seventy years spent by me among savages form the subject
of this story, but not, be it noted, seventy years of *consciousness*
that my life was so cast, for during the first part of my residence
in the strange land where I was bred, the dreadful reality of my
surroundings was hardly suspected by me, except now and then,
perhaps, in a passing glimmer of apprehension. Then, by slow
degrees, incident after incident brought a gradual awakening,
until at last there dawned on my mind the conviction which alone
could explain and reconcile for me the many contradictions of our
society — that we were not "civilized" but "savages" — that the
"dark ages," far from being part of a remote past, were very
literally present.

And here, in explanation of my long blindness to an
unwelcome truth, it must be remarked that there is a fixed and
almost insuperable superstition among my savage fellow-
islanders — and, indeed, among all the surrounding nations —
that they are a cultured and highly civilized race, living in an age
which has wholly emerged from the barbarism of their forefathers,

the "good old times" to which some of them even affect to look back with feelings of pious regretfulness. It was this delusion, to which I was at first fully subject, that made it so difficult for me to see things in their true light, and still makes it wellnigh impossible to communicate the truth to others, except to those whose suspicions have in like measure been aroused. In reality, it will be seen, the difference between the earlier "barbarism" and the later so-called "civilization" is, in the main, a mere matter of the absence or presence of certain intellectual refinements and mechanical sciences, which, while largely altering and complicating the outward conditions of life, leave its essentially savage spirit almost entirely untouched.

It was not till I was over thirty years of age that I felt any serious concern as to the manners and customs with which I was familiar, and which I had unquestioningly accepted from childhood as part of the natural order. I had heard and read of "savages," but felt the more satisfaction to know that I was a native of a land which had for centuries enjoyed the blessings of civilization and of religion, which it was anxious to disseminate as widely as possible throughout the earth. Why the diet of my countrymen should have been the first thing to set me pondering, I am unable to say, for as my later discoveries convinced me, the dietetic habits of these people are not more astonishing than many kindred practices which I still regarded without mistrust. But it was so; and I then found myself realizing, with an amazement which time has not diminished, that the "meat" which formed the staple of our diet, and which I was accustomed to regard — like bread, or fruit, or vegetables — as a mere commodity of the table, was in truth dead flesh — the actual flesh and blood — of oxen, sheep, swine, and other animals that were slaughtered in vast numbers under conditions so horrible that even to mention the subject at our dinner-tables would have been an unpardonable offence.

Now, when I began to put questions to my friends and acquaintances about this apparently glaring inconsistency in our "civilization," I could not help observing, novice though I was in such discussion, that the answers by which they sought to parry my awkward importunities were extremely evasive and sophistical — reminding me of the quibbling explanations which travellers have received from cannibals when they inquired too closely into certain dietetic observances; and from this I could not but suspect that, as far as diet was concerned, we differed in degree only from the savages whom we deemed so debased.

It must be understood, however, that here, and in other references to "savages," I use that term in its natural and inoffensive meaning, as implying simply a lack of the higher civilization and not any personal cruelty or bloodthirstiness. What I write is just a friendly account of friendly savages (by one of them); and I would emphasize the fact that the kindliness and good nature of my fellow-countrymen are in one direction quite as marked features of their character as their savagery is in another. In their own families, to their own kith and kin, to their personal friends — to all those whom fortune has placed within, instead of without the charmed circle of relationship — their conduct, in the great majority of cases, is exemplary; it is only where custom or prejudice has dug a gulf of division between their fellow-creatures and themselves that they indulge in the barbarous practices to which I refer.

It may be convenient if I here speak briefly of their other customs under two heads: first, those that relate to human beings; and, secondly, those that relate to the so-called lower animals. In few ways, perhaps, is the barbarism of these islanders more apparent than in their wars and in their preparation for wars. For what they call "peace" is, in fact, only an armed truce — an interval between two outbreaks of hostility — during which, so far from being at genuine peace with their neighbours, they are occupied in speculating where the next attack shall be delivered, or, rather (for they love to depict themselves as always standing on pious self-defence against the wanton aggressiveness of others), how they shall repel the next attack from abroad. It is their custom always to have, for the time being, some bugbear among neighbouring tribes, whose supposed machinations against the richer portions of their empire give them constant cause for unrest, and prompt them to cement undying, but equally transitory, alliances with other nations, so that their very friendships are based less on the spirit of amity than on that of distrust. Under pretence of believing in an unbelievable and, indeed, wholly ridiculous maxim — *Si vis pacem, para bellum* ("If you wish for peace, prepare for war") — they keep their minds for ever set on wars and rumours of wars, with the result that, in spite of all their profession of benevolence and brotherhood, the trade of *killing* is that which is above all others respected by them. Is money required for purposes of national welfare, such as education or the relief of the poor? Every difficulty is at once put in the way of such expenditure for such ends. But let there be the least suspicion, however irrational, of some foreign slight to "the flag," and there is scarce a savage in the island who is not willing that the public treasury should be depleted in pursuance of a childish revenge. To remonstrate against such folly is to incur the charge of being "unpatriotic."

But comical as their foreign policy is, their social system is still more so, for under the guise of "charity" and "philanthropy" there exists, in fact, a civil war, in which each individual, or group of individuals, plays a remorseless game of "Beggar my neighbour" and "Devil take the hindmost" in mad scramble for wealth; whence results, of course, a state of gross and glaring inequality, under which certain favoured persons wallow in the good things of life, while others pass their years in the pinch of extremest poverty. Thus, in due course, and by an unerring process, is manufactured what they call "the criminal class" — that is, the host of those who are driven by social injustice to outlawry and violence. And herein, perhaps, more than in any other of their customs, is shown the inherent savagery of their natures, for, instead of attempting to eradicate the *cause* of these evils by the institution of fairer and juster modes of living, my fellow-islanders are almost to a man in favour of "punishing" (that is the expression) these victims of their own foolish laws by the infliction of barbarous sentences of imprisonment, or the lash, or, in extreme cases, the gallows. To inculcate habits of honesty they shut a man in prison, and render him more than ever incapable of earning an honest livelihood. As a warning against robbery with violence, they give a lesson in official violence by flogging the criminal; and, by way of teaching the sanctity of human life, they judicially murder the murderer. Many a grotesque absurdity is solemnly and deliberately enacted in their so-called "courts of law"; and any one who ventures to suggest that this is the case is regarded as a fool and reprobate for his pains.

But it is when we turn to their treatment of the non-human races that we find the surest evidences of barbarism; yet their savagery, even here, is not wholly "naked and unashamed," for, strange to say, these curious people delight to mask their rudeness

21

in a cloak of fallacies and sophisms, and to represent themselves as "lovers" of those very creatures whom they habitually torture for "sport," "science," and the "table." They actually have a law for the prevention of cruelty to animals, under which certain privileged species, classed as "domestic," are protected from some specified wrongs, though all the time they may, under certain conditions, be subjected with impunity to other and worse injuries at the hands of the slaughterman or the vivisector; while the wild species, though presumably not less sensitive to pain, are regarded as almost entirely outside the pale of protection, and as legitimate subjects for those brutalities of "fashion" and "sport" which are characteristic of the savage mind. Their women go furred and feathered with the skins of beasts and birds; and so murderous is their millinery that whole species are sacrificed to this reckless habit. Nothing can exceed the ferocity of the national pastimes, in which, under the plea of affording healthful exercise to their tormentors, park-bred deer, that have been kept in paddocks for the purpose, are turned out before a mob of men and dogs to be baited and worried; foxes, otters, and hares are hunted and "broken up"; bagged rabbits are "coursed" in small enclosures by yelling savages on the eve of the weekly religious festival; pheasants and other "preserved" birds are mown down in thousands in an organized butchery euphemistically known as the *battue*; pigeons are released from traps in order to be shot by gangs of ruffians who gamble over the result of their skill; and almost every conceivable form of cowardly slaughter is practised as "sportsmanlike" and commended as "manly." All this, moreover, is done before the eyes and for the example of mere youths and children, who are thus from their tenderest years instructed in the habit of being pitiless and cruel. Nay, in some cases they are even encouraged to take part in such doings, and on the first occasion when they are "in at the death" are initiated by being "blooded" — that is, baptized with the blood of the slaughtered victim of their sport.

Nor are these things perhaps so strange as they might at first appear, for, in spite of their boasted progress in sciences and arts, my countrymen are still practically ignorant of the real kinship which exists between mankind and the other races, and of the duties which this kinship implies. They are still the victims of that old anthropocentric superstition which pictures Man as the centre

of the universe, and separated from the inferior animals — mere
playthings made for his august pleasure and amusement — by
a deep intervening gulf; and it is probable enough that if any one
of these unthinking savages who "break up" a hare, or baptize
their children in the blood of a butchered fox, were reminded that
he himself is in very truth an "animal," he would resent such
statement of an established fact as a slight on his religious convictions and on his personal self-respect. For, as the author of
*Hudibras* discovered:

> There's nothing so absurd, or vain,
> Or barbarous, or inhumane,
> But if it lay the least pretence
> To piety and godliness,
> And zeal for gospel truths profess,
> Does sacred instantly commence.

The very scientists themselves, who have in theory renounced
the old-fashioned idea of a universe created for mankind, are
inclined in practice to belie their own biological faith, for they
claim the moral right to devote large numbers of the lower
animals, without scruple or remorse, to the tortures of
"research," just as if the fact of a close kinship between the
vivisector who wields the scalpel and the dog who lies in the
trough were a notion of which Science is unaware!

Is it surprising that, to those of us who have gradually realized
that we are dwelling in a wild land among savages such as these,
the consciousness of the discovery should at times bring with it
a sense of unutterable loneliness and desolation — that we should
feel cut off, as it were, by interminable leagues of misunder-
standing from all human intercourse, and from all possibility of
expressing ourselves? What appeal *can* be made to people whose
first instinct, on seeing a beautiful animal, full of joyousness and
vitality, is to hunt or eat it? One can only marvel how such sheer,
untempered barbarism has come down to us from the past.

But the facts, though so terrible in their first impression, are
capable of being more hopefully regarded; there is a consolatory,
as well as a discomforting, way of interpreting them. For if these
countrymen of ours are indeed savages (as who can doubt?), have
we not at least reason to rejoice that, being savages, they in many
ways conduct themselves so discreetly, and that, as far as their
sense of relationship extends, they are so civil, so kindly, so

law-abiding? Instead, therefore, of too loudly upbraiding them for hunting or eating their little brethren, the animals, ought we not, perhaps, to feel and express some gratitude to them that they do not hunt each other — that they have not eaten *us*? Their self-restraint in many directions is, perhaps, quite as remarkable as their self-abandonment in others; and the mere fact of one's having *lived* for many years among savages is in itself a testimony to their good nature. Looked at in this light, the trouble is not so much that they are in reality savage, as that they suppose themselves to be civilized; for it is from the false garb of civilization that the misapprehension has sprung.

But, however that may be, they are, when the worst is said of them, a quaint and interesting people, and it is my earnest wish that, by the publication of this story, I may be the means of drawing to the habits of my fellow-islanders the closer attention of anthropologists. Surely, in an age when many wild tribes have been the subject of learned discourse and of missionary enterprise, it is desirable that a race which has carried into the twentieth century the primitive customs which I have described should be critically and exhaustively studied. If such should indeed be the result of this book, I shall be more than compensated for whatever pain I may have felt in the writing of these strange but faithfully recorded experiences.

*Seventy Years Among Savages*


### Homo Sapiens

What mocking elf, on impish mischief bent,
Called Man, this barbarous Man, the Sapient;
Man, who, disdainful of the nobler way,
Still lives by rapine, a dull beast of prey,
Nor spares, if so a savage gust he win,
To rob his fellows or devour his kin?
Yet nearer than he knew that jester came
To give rapacious Man the fitting name;
For change one single letter, and behold —
In "Homo Rapiens" the true tale is told!

*Cum Grano*

## SALT AND VEGETARIANISM

It is the special purpose of this book to set forth in a clear and rational manner the logic of vegetarianism.

With a view to this result, it will be convenient to have recourse now and then to the form of dialogue, so as to bring into sharper contrast the *pros* and *cons* of the argument.

From the introduction to *The Logic of Vegetarianism*

### The Raison d'Être of Vegetarianism

Behind the mere name of the reformed diet, whatever name be employed (and, as we have seen, "vegetarian" at present holds the field), lies the far more important reality. What is the *raison d'être*, the real purport of vegetarianism? Certainly not any *a priori* assumption that all animal substances, as such, are unfit for human food; for though it is quite probable that the movement will ultimately lead us to the disuse of animal products, vegetarianism is not primarily based on any such hard-and-fast formula, but on the conviction, suggested in the first place by instinctive feeling, but confirmed by reason and experience, that there are certain grave evils inseparable from the practice of flesh-eating. The aversion to flesh food is not chemical, but moral, social, hygienic. Believing as we do that the grosser forms of diet not only cause a vast amount of unnecessary suffering to the animals, but also react most injuriously on the health and morals

25

of mankind, we advocate their gradual discontinuance; and so long as this protest is successfully launched, the mere name by which it is called is a matter of minor concern. But here on this practical issue, as before on the nominal issue, we come into conflict with the superior person who, with a smile of supercilious compassion, cannot see *why* we poor ascetics should thus afflict ouselves without cause.

SUPERIOR PERSON: But why, my dear sir — why should you refuse a slice of roast beef? What is the difference between roasting an ox and boiling an egg? In the latter case you are eating an animal in embryo — that is all.

VEGETARIAN: Do you not draw any distinction between the lower and the higher organisation?

SUPERIOR PERSON: None whatever. They are chemically identical in substance.

VEGETARIAN: Possibly; but we were talking, not of chemistry, but of morals, and an egg is certainly not morally identical with an ox.

SUPERIOR PERSON: How or where does the moral phase of food-taking enter the science of dietetics?

VEGETARIAN: At a good many points, I think. One of them is the question of cannibalism. Allow me to read you a passage from the *Encyclopaedia Britannica*: "Man being by nature [?] carnivorous as well as frugivorous, and human flesh being not unfit for human food, the question arises why mankind generally have not only avoided it, but have looked with horror on exceptional individuals and races addicted to cannibalism. It is evident on consideration that both emotional and religious motives must have contributed to bring about this prevailing state of mind."

SUPERIOR PERSON: Of course. Why read me all that?

VEGETARIAN: To show you that what you call "the moral phase of food-taking" has undoubtedly affected our diet. The very thought of eating human flesh is revolting to you. Yet human flesh is chemically identical with animal flesh, and if it be true that to boil an egg is the same thing as to roast an ox, it follows that to butcher an ox is the same thing as to murder a man. Such is the logical position in which you have placed yourself by ignoring the fact that all life is not *equally* valuable, but that the higher the life the greater the responsibility incurred by those who destroy it.

Or it may be that the superior person, instead of denying that morals affect dietetics, himself poses as so austere a moralist as to scorn the wretched half-measure of merely abstaining from flesh food while still using animal products. The result is in either case the same. The all-or-nothing argument is sometimes put forward in this fashion:

SUPERIOR PERSON: Well, as far as the right or wrong of the question is concerned, I would not care to be a vegetarian at all, unless I were a thorough one. What can be the good of forswearing animal food in one form if you take it in another?

VEGETARIAN: But surely it is rational to deal with the worst abuses first. To insist on an all-or-nothing policy would be fatal to any reform whatsoever. Improvements never come in the mass, but always by instalment; and it is only reactionists who deny that half a loaf is better than no bread.

SUPERIOR PERSON: But in this case I understand that it is quite possible to be consistent. There are individuals, are there not, who live upon a purely vegetable diet, without using milk or eggs? Now, those are the people whose action one can at least appreciate and respect.

VEGETARIAN: Quite so. We fully admit that they are in advance of their fellows. We regard them as pioneers, who are now anticipating a future phase of our movement.

SUPERIOR PERSON: You admit, then, that this extreme vegetarianism is the more ideal diet?

VEGETARIAN: Yes. To do more than you have undertaken to do is a mark of signal merit; but no discredit attaches on that account to those who have done what they undertook. We hold that "the first step," as Tolstoy has expressed it, is to clear oneself of all complicity in the horrible business of the slaughter-house.

SUPERIOR PERSON: Well, I must repeat that, were I to practise any form of asceticism, I should incline to that which does not do things by halves.

VEGETARIAN: Of course. That is invariably the sentiment of those who do not do things at all.

Asceticism! Such is the strange idea with which, in many minds, our principles are associated. It would be impossible to take a more erroneous view of modern vegetarianism; and it is only through constitutional or deliberate blindness to the meaning of the movement that such a misconception can arise. How can we convey to our flesh-eating friends, in polite yet sufficiently forcible language, that their diet is an abomination to us, and that our "abstinence," far from being ascetic, is much more nearly allied to the joy that never palls? Is the farmer an ascetic because, looking over into his evil-smelling pigsty, he has no inclination to swill himself from the same trough as the swine? And why, then, should it be counted asceticism on our part to refuse, on precisely the same grounds, to eat the swine themselves? No; our opponents must clearly recognise, if they wish to form any correct notion of vegetarianism, that it is based, not on asceticism, but aestheticism; not on the mortification, but the gratification of the higher pleasures.

We conclude, then, that the cause which vegetarians have at heart is the outcome, not of some barren academic formula, but of a practical reasoned conviction that flesh food, especially butchers' meat, is a harmful and barbarous diet. Into the details of this belief we need not at present enter; it has been sufficient here to show that such belief exists, and that the good people who can see in vegetarianism nothing but a whimsical "fad" have altogether failed to grasp its true purport and significance. The *raison d'être* of vegetarianism is the growing sense that flesh-eating is a cruel, disgusting, unwholesome, and wasteful practice, and that it behoves humane and rational persons, disregarding the common cant about "consistency" and "all or nothing," to reform their diet to what extent and with what speed they can.

*The Logic of Vegetarianism*

I suggest that in proportion as man is truly "humanised," not by schools of cookery but by schools of thought, he will abandon the barbarous habit of his flesh-eating ancestors, and will make gradual progress towards a purer, simpler, more humane, and therefore more civilised diet-system.

From Introduction to *The Humanities of Diet*

### The Moralist at the Shambles

Where slaughter'd beasts lie quivering, pile on pile,
And bare-armed fleshers, bathed in bloody dew,
Ply hard their ghastly trade, and hack and hew,
And mock sweet Mercy's name, yet loathe the while
The lot that chains them to this service vile,
Their hands in hideous carnage to imbrue:
Lo, there!—the preacher of the Good and True,
The Moral Man, with sanctimonious smile!

"Thrice happy beasts," he murmurs, "'tis our love,
Our thoughtful love, that sends you to the knife
(Nay, doubt not, as ye welter in your gore!);
For thus alone ye earned the boon of life,
And thus alone the Moralist may prove
His sympathetic soul—by eating more!"

*The Humanities of Diet*

### Grace Before Meat

What fairer sight can earth afford
Than welcome friends round festive board,
With pious grace before their meat?—
*For what we are about to eat,*
    *God make us truly thankful!*

For soup, concocted from the tails
Of oxen dragged from distant vales,
Till over-driven, bruised and sore,
They stumbled to the shambles' door:—
    *God make us truly thankful!*

For cutlets, delicately white—
A calf it was that gambol'd light,
Then, taken from its mother's side,
Was slowly bled, and bleeding died:—
    *God make us truly thankful!*

A turkey next, from dunghill reft,
With sausages to right and left;
Sliced ham, the flesh of measly swine:—
*God spare the health of those who dine,*
    *And make them truly thankful!*

But here we pause; 'twere long to tell
What corpses still the banquet swell;
Yea, all that land and sea produce:—
*God bless these creatures to our use,*
    *And make us truly thankful!*

*The Humanities of Diet*

### The Village Butcher
(after Longfellow)

Under a spreading chestnut tree
The village shambles stand;
The butcher—busy man is he,
With pole-axe in his hand,
And a meaning look about his eye
That cattle understand.

His coat is loose, and blue, and long,
His face is like the tan;
His brow is wet with more than sweat;
He kills whate'er he can,
And looks the whole world in the face,
Like an honest slaughterman.

And children, coming home from school,
Peep eager through the door;
They love to see the slaughtered sheep,
And hear the bullocks roar,
And watch the dying pigs that lie
A-kicking on the floor.

Hacking, whacking, slaughtering,
Onward through life he goes.
Each morn the living beasts come in,
Each night they hang in rows:
Murder attempted, murder done,
Has earned him sweet repose.


Thanks, thanks, to thee, my gory friend,
For the lesson thou has taught;
Thus from the reeking slaughterhouse,
Our British beef is brought.
"Old England's beef!" No more for me:
I relish not the thought!
*The Humanities of Diet*

### St. Horsley and The Snail

"It is a wicked waste of food to see great big snails
crawling about unmolested and uneaten." — Canon Horsley

When Horsley saw his native land
    By great big snails infested,
Like scaly dragons in a band
    Marauding unmolested;
True warrior-saint, he smote the foe,
    But, not content to beat him,
"Come, friends," he cried to high and low,
    "He's edible—let's eat him."

Ah, wise advice, precluding waste!
    Sound, practical, convincing!
Boiled slugs, to charm the public taste,
    Made daintier by mincing!
Small wonder, 'neath this rival star,
    Saint George's fame is paling:
A dragon? Pooh! Sport's finer far
    When Horsley goes a-snailing.

*The Humanities of Diet*

31

## SALT AND SOCIALISM

[The capitalist classes] insist that they are the rightful possessors of wealth which comes in to them without any labour on their part, and attempt to raise the cry of 'Stop thief' against those who venture even to investigate the origin of their wealth. Our capitalists persist to the bitter end in the fatuous assertion that to live idly on the labour of others is not the same thing as to steal.

"Thou Shalt Not Steal," *Justice*, March 14, 1885

### Some Misapprehensions

One of the most amusing conceits now current among the well-to-do classes is their fond belief that they are entitled to look back with a smile of superior enlightenment upon the "languorous and woolly-brained" age which they call the Victorian. That in the last quarter-century there have been many important mechanical inventions, and some startling but quite superficial changes in manners and fashions, is beyond doubt; but as far as society's intellectual progress is concerned, it is difficult to see what ground exists for the present mood of self-satisfaction. The mental ascendancy of Georgian over Victorian, is in no field very apparent; least of all in regard to labour questions; indeed, the amazing flood of nonsense about Socialism poured forth at every election, suffices in itself to show that there is still as much need as ever to echo the cry of a Victorian poet: "More brain, O Lord, more brain."

Why is it that, as a result of a century of enormously increased production of wealth, owing to its use of labour-saving machinery, the country is still faced by the spectacle of a glaring inequality in the condition of those who have created that wealth — on the one hand, great riches in the possession of a few, on the other, poverty, or the dread of poverty, as the lifelong lot of the many? That is the question which has called into existence the movement known to us as Socialism, the question which was thus asked, and answered, by another Victorian writer:

> "Why do people die of starvation, or lead a miserable existence on the verge of it? Why have millions upon millions to toil from morning to evening just to gain a mere crust of bread?
>
> "Because of the absolute lack of organisation by which such labour should produce its effects, the absolute lack of distribution, the absolute lack even of the very idea that such things are possible. Nay, even to mention such things, to say that they are possible, is criminal with many."*

That many evade the inquiry, as if they thought it almost criminal, is evident from the fact that the ethical purpose of Socialism — no less than its economics — is so widely misunderstood. Indeed, most criticisms seem to be concerned not with what Socialism is, but with what Socialism is not.

Among the various characters gracefully delineated by Tennyson is that of a certain Edmund, in "The Brook," a poetic youth who was unable to understand "how money breeds," yet himself, by his creative imagination, could make —

> "The thing that is not as the thing that is."

The picture is a pretty one; but it must be owned that there are nowadays not a few very prosaic persons who, while they fully understand how money breeds — and themselves breed it very successfully — also possess, though in a somewhat different sense, the imaginative and inventive faculty; indeed, when Socialism is the subject, the number of platform Edmunds, journalistic Edmunds, dinner-table Edmunds, and lecturing Edmunds, engaged in presenting the thing that is not as the thing that is, leaves the efforts of the original Edmund quite outclassed.

But when one considers that the great majority of well-to-do Englishmen have in very truth never heard anything about Socialism except from its opponents, and that their opinion of it has been mainly formed through the daily and weekly

*From *The Story of My Heart*, by Richard Jefferies, 1883.

comments of a hostile press, written in many cases by writers whose ignorance almost equals that of their readers, it is not surprising that there should be widespread misapprehension not only of the practical aims of Socialism, but of the underlying principles by which it is inspired. It is of less consequence, perhaps, that many deluded citizens should still be dreading the day when a Socialist Government will divide all property equally among its rapacious supporters ("Why, they'll take my house away!" was a remark lately made to me by a troubled elector), because time may be trusted to show the absurdity of such fears; but it is a serious matter that a movement whose very name implies a sense of brotherhood should be regarded as a gospel of robbery and hatred.

Yet such is the view of Socialism which still is prevalent, and in some quarters sedulously fostered to-day. The impression is of a host of greedy "Have-nots," banded together in a desperate alliance with foreign revolutionists, to confiscate the hard-earned property of the more diligent "Haves," reckless of the great truth, the basis of society, that the fruits of a man's labour should be his own. Such is the picture; and those who are not aware of its falseness may be pardoned if, with so dismal a prospect before them, they raise the cry of "Confiscation!"

Now there are wild men in all parties (not least among self-styled constitutionalists); and with Socialism taking many forms in many countries, it was inevitable that the lurid variety of it should in some quarters find expression in terms of hatred and violence which, if they stood alone, might be held to justify what is, in general, a mere misrepresentation and caricature. But if we would judge rightly of any social movement, we must view it in its best, not its worst aspect; and no one who has had any wide acquaintance with Socialists, either personally or through their writings, could recognise the cause to which many lives are being unselfishly devoted in that imaginary campaign of hatred and rapine which is a terror to many persons who know no better, and is used as a convenient bugbear by some who do.

For to begin with, Socialism does not advocate "confiscation." It seems to be overlooked that the Socialist doctrine had its origin not among ignorant and poverty-stricken folk who could only regard the matter in a mood of passion, but in the minds of quiet thinkers who had no personal interests at stake and were influenced

34

solely by a sense of equity and justice. That the measures advocated by Socialists are by some persons *thought* to be confiscation, is true enough; but to assert that Socialists themselves approve of confiscation is merely to beg the question at issue in a very childish manner.

"The fruits of a man's labour should be his own." Of course; but it is necessary to know what *are* the fruits of a man's labour. It is the Socialist contention that under the present capitalist system the working classes do not enjoy the full fruits of their labour, but that a large portion of those fruits is filched from them through highly-complicated processes which it is the province of the economist to explain. The demand, therefore, is not for "confiscation," but rather for the restoration of "stolen goods," and for what Socialists believe to be a juster and more righteous system. Reject this claim if you will, but do not pretend that it is a dishonest one because it conflicts with your own. The case must be decided by some higher authority than either of the parties to the dispute, and it is to that higher authority, public opinion (for there is no other), that Socialists appeal.

What right have the moneyed classes to brand such an appeal as an attempt at "robbery"? In a dispute, to which there are necessarily two parties, claimant and defendant, is the defendant to be allowed to play also the part of arbitrator, to dismiss his adversary's plea as factious and dishonest, while he himself leaves the court (and the Bench) "without a stain upon his character." For that, without exaggeration, is the attitude assumed by the many pompous gentlemen who denounce Socialism as preaching "hatred and class war," themselves forgetting that, as it needs two to make a quarrel, so in like manner, a class war can only be made when there are two parties to it, and that the folk who are charged with holding more than their just share of the good things of life, yet refuse to accept arbitration, are just as responsible for the outbreak of a class war, indeed, more so, than those by whom the appeal is lodged.*

---

*Here is a salient example. Lord Londonderry, himself the owner of thousands of acres, presiding at a meeting of the National Conservative League, remarked that "the National Conservative League was the negation of class hatred and class warfare." (*The Observer*, Jan. 4, 1925.) What can one do but exclaim, with Dominie Sampson, "Prodigious!"

And as for the "hatred," that too will depend upon circumstances and the temperaments of those concerned. Hatred is not necessarily a characteristic of one party rather than of the other. If there are Socialists who hate "the Capitalist", there are also Capitalists, great and small, whose hatred of "the agitator" is quite as freely avowed, and in language as well able to hold its own, if vituperation-matches were included in the programme of the Olympic games. But there are also calm minds, who can affirm and maintain their case dispassionately; and these are certainly not lacking on the Socialist side more than on the other.

It must be remembered, too, that class hatred may show itself in many and various forms, not always of a violent kind. Much was said at the time of the last General Election of attempts by "roughs" to prevent free speech at Conservative meetings; but apart from the fact that some Socialist candidates also suffered in that way, how, but as signs of malignant and deep-seated hatred, were we to regard the innumerable lying cartoons, grossly insulting not only to political opponents but to a great foreign nation, with which the "patriotic" party did not scruple to disfigure the walls of every village and town? Whatever offence the "roughs" may have committed, it was at least less dastardly than that which the "smooths," if the term may be permitted (and we have heard of smooth-faced assassins), seemed to regard as part of their day's business at election time.

Let us begin, then, by putting hypocrisy out of our path, and by recognising that, whatever conclusion may ultimately be reached, the issue raised by Socialism is quite plain and outspoken. The distribution of wealth, under a capitalist system, is arraigned as unjust to the workers and injurious to the best interests of the community; but it is not to be assumed either that the present holders of wealth are consciously dishonest, or that there is dishonesty in the Socialist claim.

Here the moneyed man may object that, even if the personal integrity of Socialists be admitted, their practical intent is to deprive him in some degree of the property that he has earned or inherited; in a word, to rob him of "his own." Now no sane person (for criminals cannot be reckoned as sane) desires to rob a fellow-being of his own. The whole question turns on the definition of "one's own"; and if it be the case that some citizens have acquired more than can fairly be included in that term, or are using their wealth tyrannically, the State has evidently the right to intervene. There would be no more "robbery" in such readjustment than in the levying of income-tax; and the rational course of the property-holder is not to abuse Socialism, but to satisfy himself and his conscience as to the origin and nature of his estate.

Must we all, then, devote much time to the study of political economy, that abstruse science which, far from being what some have unkindly termed it, a "dismal" one, is of so sprightly and versatile a character that its lifelong professors seem to differ among themselves almost as much in the end as at the beginning? This is a matter of which I cannot speak from experience, for I have never succeeded in the conscientious attempt to read the works of the learned economists from their forefather, the first Adam (Smith), downward; but I venture to suggest that for the truth-seekers who are content with something less than a scientific exposition of such complex and elusive inquiries as those concerned with the sources of wealth and the value of labour, a much simpler form of personal introspection may suffice. The saying that every man is a fool or a physician at forty can be applied with equal advantage in other branches of thought.

For example, if any one of those who, like myself (and their number is legion) have lived for years on an unearned or partly unearned income, would submit to the heart-searching question, how, and by whose exertions, he is housed, clothed, fed, and generally maintained in comfort, I think the speculation might be a profitable one. For though man shall not live by bread alone, he shall not live without bread, nor without the other numerous commodities with which every well-to-do household provides itself; and these, obviously, are being produced by *some* persons' labour. That we are being supported by involuntary contributions is beyond doubt. Who those contributors are, and why they are so obliging as to supply our daily and yearly wants, is a question that has long presented itself for my consideration. In other words, how much of what I legally possess, is, veritably, and in equity my own?

It is the intricacy of the problem, the extreme subtlety of the various channels through which wealth is drained away from one quarter to another, that makes a precise solution very difficult, and so obscures the truth; for if even economists cannot agree among themselves as to all the details of their science, how can the layman expect a mathematical answer to his questionings? Yet the main fact is clear beyond dispute, that it is because the workman — compelled to make what terms he may with those who can permit or deny him the necessary access to the land or to the means of production — does not receive the full value of his toil, that there is a surplus which serves to provide an "income" for a host of "employers" and "investors." Every *plus*, as Ruskin expressed it, has its *minus*; and those who do not bear their full part in some productive occupation, are living to that extent on the labour of others. That in many cases it is not easy to estimate the exact amount of their indebtedness does not in the least invalidate the general truth of this statement, which is the central tenet of Socialism.

And mark: this unearned "income," this incoming stream of dividends, whose exact source, like that of some underground river, is partly a matter of conjecture, does not cease with the life of its present owner or with the life of his successor, but flows on perpetually, like that brook of Tennyson's, which conversed so candidly with Edmund.

> "For men may come and men may go,
> But I go on for ever."

What folly, then, to pretend that there would be any "robbery" or "confiscation," if, at some point in its course where least personal hardship could result, this flood of surplus wealth were gradually* diverted from private to public channels, instead of being permitted, as now, to roll on from generation to generation, forever enriching the few at the cost of the many! To plead that the capital thus acquired is benefiting the workers themselves, by being used in furthering employment, is obviously beside the point, because it would have the same beneficial effect if it belonged to the State, with the advantage that the profits would be not personal but communal.

For these reasons, it is incumbent on truth-seekers to desist from mere abuse of those who are striving towards fairer social

---

*Opponents of Socialism, as of other reforms, frequently talk of the disruption that would be caused by a sudden change, as if it were proposed to turn everything upside-down the day after to-morrow. On the contrary, the transformation would be effected progressively, by degrees, unless prolonged obstruction precipitated matters, a result for which the "die-hards" would have only themselves to blame.

conditions, and to apply themselves to a more serious consideration of the matter that is in debate, as may easily be done by stu-
dying one of the popular expositions of Socialism.* With ready
access to an understanding of the thing that *is*, there is no possible
excuse for a continued denunciation of the thing that is *not*; it
is somewhat rash, too, to raise the ancient cry of "stop thief,"
unless you have first taken the precaution to look in your own
pockets. Even the most respectable of us may, unconsciously, be
addicted to kleptomania.

From the sole point of view of the wealthy classes and their
dependents, it were surely better to learn what Socialism means,
and then, if so minded, to use that knowledge for its frustration,
than to go on repeating idle cries and shibboleths which are the
outcome of mere ignorance, and which, after half-a-century's constant service, are wearing somewhat thin.

*E.g., "The Case for Socialism," by Fred Henderson, or "The Meaning of
Socialism," by J. Bruce Glasier (I.L.P., 14, Great George Street, Westminster).
Mr. Henderson's book is written with extreme perspicuity; and no one who reads
even the two opening chapters of it can fail to rid his mind of the common
misunderstandings.

*The Heart of Socialism*

[A]mong the many ponderous fallacies in which the opponents
of Socialism entrench themselves, there are some which seem to
be best attacked by ridicule, and by that form of ridicule which
finds expression in verse. Our inert modern "Respectability,"
which is, in fact, ancient Rascality padded out with sawdust —
as heartless and less honest — is a fitting mark for epigram; and
here, perhaps, service may be rendered by the lightly-armed
versifier, who, without making claim to the sterner function of
the satirist, can occasionally turn a rhyme and overturn a fool.

From introduction to *The Song of the Respectables, and Other Verses*

### The Song of the Respectables

Respectables are we,
And we fain would have you see
Why we confidently claim to be respected;
In well-ordered homes we dwell,
And discharge our duties well—
Well dressed, well bred, well mannered, well connected.

We hate the common cant
About poverty and want,
And all that is distressing and unhealthy;
Certain cases may be sad,
But the system can't be bad,
If it gives such satisfaction to the wealthy.

As the *Times* each day we read,
We realise the need
Of more and more repression for the Masses;
And we muse with wondering awe
On the sanctity of Law,
As administered and construed by the Classes.

To us the breath of Change
Is ominous and strange,
And Reform is but a cloak for Revolution;
Our concern is not for self,
Not for property nor pelf,
Oh no, but for the British Constitution:

And our care transcends e'en that,
For in sable coat and hat
We never fail to flock to church each Sunday,
That with renovated zest,
And conscience lulled to rest,
We may yield our hearts to Mammon on the Monday.

So our wealth, which swells apace,
Is the outward sign of grace,
As property goes step by step with piety:
In the present world we thrive,
Then save our souls alive,
And move for evermore in good society.

Thus on through life we march,
Stiff with decency and starch,
Well bred, well fed, well mannered, well connected—
For Respectables are we,
And you cannot fail to see
Why we confidently claim to be respected.

*The Song of the Respectables, and Other Verses*

### Those Idle Poor

Those idle Poor! We know their ways,
As thriftless as could be:—
Yet who, I wonder, all my days,
Has clothed and nurtured *me*?
So volatile, their tasks they shirk;
Go sporting each spare minute,
While million men are out of work:—
And *I* was never in it.
Such wasters surely should be sent
As emigrants o'ersea:—
But if too many of them went,
What would become of *me*?
Their recklessness we rich deplore,
Their profligacy pains us:—
And yet (a thought that makes me sore)
Their labour still sustains us!

*Cum Grano*

### "On the Dole"

"The dole!" 'Tis shame. For manhood's sake
Your heart is sore concerned:
You blush to see yon claimants take
Their niggard wage unearned.
Nay, chafe not thus, my noble friend;
Your virtuous rage control!
*You* draw your unearned dividend:—
You, too, are "on the dole."

*Cum Grano*

41

## A Song of Freedom
### Dedicated to the Liberty and Property Defence League

I marvel that no poet sings
    Of "Individual Freedom."
And what unnumbered gifts she brings
    To all save those who need 'em.

Her choicest favours fall, we see,
    On this enfranchised nation;
Free contract, competition free,
    Free trade, and free starvation.

Here dwells the freedom of the Press;
    Free speech, and free replying;
Here orators are free; well, yes,
    They're free enough in lying.

Here surely is the age of gold,
    The land of milk and honey,
Where everything is freely sold
    To all who have the money.

We British workmen, so they say,
    Are free; and who can doubt it?
For if we do not like our pay,
    We're free to go without it.

Unlike the helpless negro slave,
    Our tyrant-driven brother,
If one employer prove a knave,
    We're free to find another.

To travel, too, we can afford,
    With this slight limitation,
That though we're free to step on board,
    They call it emigration.

Or, if we dread this life-long flight,
    And vow our homes to cherish,
We have an immemorial right
    To stay behind and perish.

So, hey! for England's glorious rights,
  Free selling and free buying,
Free libraries, free pews, free fights,—
  And a free ditch to die in!
*The Song of the Respectables, and Other Verses*

## SALT AND THE HUMANITARIAN LEAGUE

### Manifesto of the Humanitarian League

The Humanitarian League has been established on the basis of an intelligible and consistent principle of humaneness — that it is iniquitous to inflict suffering, directly or indirectly, on any sentient being, except when self-defence or absolute necessity can be justly pleaded.

This principle the Humanitarian League will apply and emphasise in those cases where it appears to be most flagrantly overlooked, and will protest not only against the cruelties inflicted by men on men, in the name of law, authority, and conventional usage, but also (in accordance with the same sentiment of humanity) against the wanton ill-treatment of the lower animals.

The Humanitarian League will therefore propose a thorough revision and more equitable administration of the present Criminal Code, under which a very large amount of injustice and oppression is constantly perpetrated.

43

It will deprecate the various provocations and incentives to aggressive warfare, and will point to the evils that result from the ever-increasing array of military and naval armaments.

It will inculcate the public duty of affording protection to the weak and helpless, and will urge the need of amending the present social conditions, under which a large portion of the people is in a state of chronic destitution.

It will contend that the practice of vivisection is incompatible with the fundamental principles both of humanity and sound science, and that the infliction of suffering for ends purely selfish, such as sport, fashion, profit, or professional advancement, has been largely instrumental in debasing the general standard of morality.

Furthermore, the Humanitarian League will aim at the prevention of the terrible sufferings to which animals are subjected in the cattle-traffic and the shambles, and will advocate, as an initial measure, the abolition of *private* slaughter-houses, the presence of which in our large centres is a cause of wide-spread demoralisation.

The Humanitarian League will look to its members to do their utmost, both in private and public, to promote the above-mentioned scheme. Its work will involve no sort of opposition to that of any existing institution; on the contrary, it is designed to supplement and reinforce such efforts as have already been organised for similar objects. The distinctive purpose and guiding policy of the League will be to consolidate and give consistent expression to those principles of humaneness, the recognition of which is essential to the understanding and realisation of all that is highest and best in Humanity.

### A League of Humaneness

Hommes, soyez humains. C'est votre premier devoir. Quelle sagesse y a-t-il pour vous, hors de l'humanité.—ROUSSEAU.

. . . Thirty years ago there were already in existence a number of societies which aimed at the humanizing of public opinion, in regard not to war only but to various other savage and uncivilized practices. The Vegetarian Society, founded in 1847, advocated a radical amendment; and the cause of zoophily, represented by the

Royal Society for the Prevention of Cruelty to Animals, had been strengthened by the establishment of several Anti-Vivisection Societies. In like manner the philanthropic tendencies of the time, with respect to prison management and the punishment or reclamation of offenders, were reflected in the work of the Howard Association.

The purpose of the Humanitarian League, which was formed in 1891, was to proclaim a *general* principle of humaneness, as underlying the various disconnected efforts, and to show that though the several societies were necessarily working on separate lines, they were nevertheless inspired and united by a single bond of fellowship. The promoters of the League saw clearly that barbarous practices can be philosophically condemned on no other ground than that of the broad democratic sentiment of universal sympathy. Humanity and science between them have exploded the time-honoured idea of a hard-and-fast line between white man and black man, rich man and poor man, educated man and uneducated man, good man and bad man: equally impossible to maintain, in the light of newer knowledge, is the idea that there is any difference in kind, and not in degree only, between human and non-human intelligence. The emancipation of men from cruelty and injustice will bring with it in due course the emancipation of animals also. The two reforms are inseparably connected, and neither can be fully realized alone.

We were well aware that a movement of this character would meet with no popular support; on the contrary, that those who took part in it would be regarded as "faddists" and "visionaries"; but we knew also that the direct opposite of this was the truth, and that while we were supposed to be merely building "castles in the air," we were in fact following Thoreau's most practical advice, and *putting the foundations under them*. For what is "the basis of morality," as laid down by so great a thinker as Schopenhauer, except this very doctrine of a comprehensive and reasoned sympathy?

A year or two before the founding of the League, I had read at a meeting of the Fabian Society a paper on "Humanitarianism," which afterwards formed a starting-point for the League's publications. The idea of a humane society, with a wider scope than that of any previously existing body, was suggested by Mr. Howard Williams; and it was at the house of a very true friend of our cause, Mrs. Lewis (now Mrs. Drakoules), in Park Square, London, that a small group of persons, among whome were Mrs. Lewis, Mr. Edward Maitland, Mr. Howard Williams, Mr. Kenneth Romanes, and the present writer,* assembled, early in 1891, to draw up a manifesto and to launch the Humanitarian League. The title "humanitarian" was chosen because, though fully aware of certain objections to the word, we felt that it was the only term which sufficiently expressed our meaning, and that, whether a good name or a bad name, it must be taken up, like a gauntlet, by those who intended to fight for the cause which it denotes.

For it was to be a fighting, not a talking Society that the League was designed, even if it were a forlorn hope. In an interesting letter, read at the first meeting, the opinion was expressed by our veteran friend, Professor Francis W. Newman, that the time was not ripe for such a venture as the assertion of a humanitarian ethic; but we came to the conclusion that however small a beginning might be made, much good would be done by a systematic protest against the numerous barbarisms of the age — the cruelties inflicted by men on men, and the still more atrocious ill-treatment of the lower animals.

Edward Maitland, who, in spite of his advanced years, took a good deal of interest in our meetings, had had rather a remarkable career as traveller, writer, and mystic; and his earlier book, *The Pilgrim and the Shrine*, had been widely read. Those who knew him only as occultist would have been surprised to see how extremely critical he was — to the verge of fastidiousness — in discussing practical affairs; there was no one on that committee more useful in bringing the cold light of reason to bear on our consultations than the joint-author of Dr. Anna Kingsford's very strange revelations. At the time I knew him, he was writing his *magnum opus*, the life of Anna Kingsford, and he would often discourse to me freely, after a committee meeting, on his spiritual experiences, to the astonishment, perhaps, of our fellow-travellers by rail or tram: on one occasion he described to me on the top of an omnibus how he had been privileged to be a beholder of the Great White Throne. There was something in these narrations

---

*Here perhaps I had better say that my own work for the League, though mostly private and anonymous, was continuous during the twenty-nine years of the League's existence; so that in describing the various aspects of the movement I am writing of what I know. The opinions expressed are, of course, only personal . . .

so natural and genuine as to compel the respectful attention of the listener, whatever his personal belief might be as to the reality of the visions described.

Mr. Howard Williams, on the other hand, was as pronounced a rationalist as Maitland was a mystic, and one who by word and by pen, in private and in public, was a quiet but untiring champion of the humanitarian cause. His *Ethics of Diet*, which had the honour, at a later date, of being highly commended by Tolstoy, whose essay entitled "The First Step" was written as a preface to his Russian translation of the book, is a veritable mine of knowledge, which ranges over every period of history and covers not only the subject of humane dietetics but the whole field of man's attitude toward the non-human races: if Ethical Societies were intended to be anything more than places of debate, they would long ago have included this work among their standard text-books. For the writing of such a treatise, Mr. Williams was specially qualified by the fact that with a wide classical knowledge he united in a remarkable degree the newer spirit and enthusiasm of humanity; he was in the truest sense a student and professor of *literae humaniores*. It is difficult to estimate precisely the result of labours such as his; but that they have had an appreciable influence upon the growth of a more humane public opinion is not to be doubted.

The Committee was gradually strengthened by the inclusion of such experienced workers as the Rev. J. Stratton, Colonel W. Lisle B. Coulson, Mrs. L. T. Mallet, Mr. J. Frederick Green, Miss Elizabeth Martyn, the first secretary of the League, and Mr. Ernest Bell, a member of the well-known publishing firm and now President of the Vegetarian Society, who for over twenty years was a bulwark of strength as chairman and treasurer. A campaign against the Royal Buckhounds had at once commanded respect; the pamphlets were well noticed in the press — better, perhaps, in those days, when they were still a novelty, than later, when they were taken as a matter of course — some successful meetings were held, and the general interest shown in the League's doings was out of all proportion to its numerical strength.

It was in 1895 that the second phase of the League's career began with the acquirement of an office in Great Queen Street, and the institution of a monthly journal, *Humanity*, so-called at first because its later title, *The Humanitarian*, was at that time appropriated elsewhere. The holding of a National Humanitarian Conference, at St. Martin's Town Hall, in the same year, was the first big public effort that the League had made, and attracted a good deal of attention; and the scope of the work was considerably extended by the appointment of special departments for dealing with such subjects as Sports, Criminal Law and Prison Reform, Humane Diet and Dress, and the Education of Children; and by a much wider use of the press as a medium for propaganda, in which sphere the League was now able to avail itself of the services of Mr. Joseph Collinson, whose numerous press letters soon became a distinctive feature of its work. In the summer of 1897 the League shifted its headquarters to Chancery Lane, where it remained till it was brought to an end in 1919.

The League was soon engaged in controversies of various kinds. A little book entitled *Animals' Rights*, which I wrote at the request of my friend, Mr. Ernest Bell, and which was published by his firm in 1892, led to a great deal of discussion, and passed through numerous editions, besides being translated into French, German, Dutch, Swedish, and other languages. Among its earliest critics was Professor D. G. Ritchie, who, in his work on *Natural Rights*, maintained that though "we may be said to have duties of *kindness towards* the animals, it is incorrect to represent these as strictly *duties towards* the animals themselves, as if they had rights against us." (The italics are Mr. Ritchie's.) There is a puzzle for you, reader. I took it to mean that in man's duty of kindness, it is the kindness only that has reference to the animals, the duty being a private affair of the man's; the convenience of which arrangement is that the man can shut off the kindness whenever it suits him to do so, the kindness being, as it were, the water, and the duty the tap. For instance, when the question of vivisection arose, Mr. Ritchie at once turned off the water of kindness, though it had been very liberally turned on by him when he gave approval to the humanitarian protests against the barbarities of sport.

To this sophistical hair-splitting, in a matter of much practical importance, we from the first refused to yield, and made it plain that it was no battle of words in which we were engaged but one of ethical conduct, and that while we were quite willing to exchange the term "rights" for a better one, if better could be found, we would not allow the concept either of human "duties" or of animals' "rights" to be manipulated in the manner of which Mr. Ritchie's book gave a conspicuous example. Meanwhile the word "rights" held the field.

The old Catholic school was, of course, antagonistic to the recognition of animals' rights, and we had controversies with Monsignor John S. Vaughan, among other sacerdotalist writers, when he laid down the ancient proposition that "beasts exist for the use and benefit of man." It may be doubted whether argument is not a pure waste of time, when there is a fundamental difference of opinion as to data and principles: the sole reason for such debate was to ensure that the humanitarian view of the question was rightly placed before the public, and to show how strange was the alliance between sacerdotalist and vivisector. Evolutionary science has demonstrated beyond question the kinship of all sentient life; yet the scientist, in order to rake together a moral defence for his doings, condescends to take shelter under the same plea as the theologian, and having got rid of the old anthropocentric fallacy in the realm of science avails himself of that fallacy in the realm of ethics: a progressive in one branch of thought, he is still a medievalist in another.

Thus scientist and sacerdotalist between them would perpetuate the experimental tortures of the laboratory. *Laborare est orare* was the old saying; now it should be expanded by the Catholic school of vivisectionists into *laboratorium est oratorium*: the house of torture is the house of prayer. It is a beautiful and touching scene of reconciliation, this meeting of priest and professor over the torture-trough of the helpless animal. They might exclaim in Tennyson's words:

> There above the little grave,
> O there above the little grave,
> We kissed again with tears.

More exhilarating was the discussion when Mr. G. K. Chesterton entered the lists as champion of those high prerogatives of Mankind, which he saw threatened by the sinister devices of humanitarians, who, as he has explained in one of his books, "uphold the claims of all creatures against those of humanity." A debate with Mr. Chesterton took place in the Essex Hall; and for several years afterwards the argument was renewed at times, as, for instance, when reviewing a book of mine on *The Logic of*

*Vegetarianism,* he insisted* that "the difference between our moral relation to men and to animals is not a difference of degree in the least: it is a difference of kind." The human race, he held, is a definite society, different from everything else. "The man who breaks a cat's back breaks a cat's back. The man who breaks a man's back breaks an implied treaty." To us, this terse saying of Mr. Chesterton's seemed to contain unintentionally the root of all cruelty to animals, the quintessence of anthropocentric arrogance. The man who breaks a cat's back, breaks a cat's back. Yes, and the scientist who vivisects a dog, vivisects a dog; the sportsman who breaks up a hare, breaks up a hare. That is all. The victims are not human. But it is a distinction which has caused, in savage hands, the immemorial ill-usage of the lower animals through the length and breadth of the world.

Perhaps the strangest of Mr. Chesterton's charges against humanitarians was one which he made in his book *Orthodoxy,* that their trend is "to touch fewer and fewer things," i.e. to abstain from one action after another until they are left in a merely negative position. He failed to see that while we certainly desire to touch fewer and fewer things with whip, hob-nailed boot, hunting-knife, scalpel, or pole-axe, we equally desire to get into touch with more and more of our fellow-beings by means of that sympathetic intelligence which tells us that they are closely akin to ourselves. Why, ultimately, do we object to such practices as vivisection, blood-sports, and butchery? Because of the cruelty inseparable from them, no doubt; but also because of the hateful narrowing of our own human pleasures which these barbarous customs involve. A recognition of the rights of animals implies no sort of disparagement of human rights: this indeed was clearly indicated in the sub-title of my book, *Animals' Rights* "considered in relation to social progress."

During the winter of 1895 – 96, a course of lectures on "Rights," as viewed from various standpoints — Christian, ethical, secularist, scientific, theosophical, and humanitarian — was organized by the Humanitarian League; and of these perhaps the most significant was Mr. Frederic Harrison's address on the ethical view, in which it was maintained that "man's morality towards the lower animals is a vital and indeed fundamental part

*Daily News,* April 10, 1906.

of his morality towards his fellow-men." At this same meeting some discussion arose on the far from unimportant question of nomenclature, objection being taken to Mr. Harrison's use of the term "brute," which he, on his part, defended as being scientifically correct, and, in the sense of "inarticulate," wholly void of offence, even when applied to such highly intelligent beings as the elephant, the horse, or the dog. Humanitarians, however, have generally held that the meaning of the word "brute," in this connection, is not "inarticulate" but "irrational," and that for this reason it should be discarded, on the ground that to call an animal a brute, or irrational, is the first step on the path to treating him accordingly. "Give a dog a bad name," says the proverb; and directly follows the injunction: "and hang him."

For like reasons the Humanitarian League always looked with disfavour on the expression "dumb animals," because, to begin with, animals are not dumb, and secondly, nothing more surely tends to their depreciation than thus to attribute to them an unreal deficiency or imperfection: such a term may be meant to increase our pity, but in the long run it lessens what is more important, our respect. In this matter the League was glad to have the support of Mr. Theodore Watts-Dunton, who, as long ago as 1877, had written satirically in the *Athenaeum* of what he called "the great human fallacy" conveyed in the words "the dumb animals," and had pointed out that animals are no more dumb than men are. Years afterwards he wrote to me to inquire about the authorship of an article in the *Humanitarian* in which the same conclusion was reached, and expressed his full sympathy with our point of view.

But much more difficult to contend with than any anti-humanitarian arguments is the dull dead weight of that unreasoning prejudice which cannot see consanguinity except in the conventional forms, and simply does not comprehend the statement that "the animals" are our fellow-beings. There are numbers of good and kindly folk with whom, on this question, one never reaches the point of difference at all, but is involved in impenetrable misapprehensions: there may be talking on either side, but communication there is none. Tell them, in Howard Moore's words, that the non-human beings are "not conveniences but cousins," and they will answer, assentingly, that they are all in favour of "kindness to animals"; after which they will continue to treat them not as cousins but as conveniences. This impossibility of even making oneself intelligible was brought home to me with great force, some years ago, in connection with the death of a very dear friend, a cat, whose long life of fifteen years had to be ended in the chloroform-box owing to an incurable ailment. The veterinary surgeon whose aid I invoked was an extremely kind man, for whose skill I shall always feel grateful; and from his patience and sympathetic manner I thought he partly understood what the occasion meant to me — that, like a human death-bed, it was a scene that could never pass from the mind. It was, therefore, with something of an amused shock that I recollected, after he had gone, what I had hardly noticed at the moment, that he had said to me, as he left the door: "You'll be wanting a new pussy-cat soon."

Richard Jefferies has remarked that the belief that animals are devoid of reason is rarely held by those who themselves labour in the fields: "It is the cabinet-thinkers who construct a universe of automatons." One is cheered now and then by hearing animals spoken of, quite simply and naturally, as rational beings. I once made the acquaintance, in the Lake District, of an old lady living in a roadside cottage, who had for her companion, sitting in an armchair by the fire, a lame hen, named Tetty, whom she had saved and reared from chicken-hood. Some years later, as I passed that way, I called and inquired after Tetty, but learnt that she was dead. "Ah, poor Tetty!" said the dame, as tears fell from her eyes; "she passed away several months ago, quite conscious to the end." That to attribute to a dying bird the self-consciousness which is supposed to be the special prerogative of mankind, should, to the great majority of persons, appear nothing less than comical, is a measure of the width of that gulf which religion has delved between "the beasts that perish" and the Christian with his "soul" to save.

But it is not often that one hears of a case like that of Tetty: as a rule, disappointment lurks in the hopes that flatter the humanitarian mind. We had a neighbour in Surrey, an old woman living in an adjoining cottage, who professed full adherence to our doctrine that cats should not be allowed to torture captured birds. "I always take them away from my cat: I can't bear to see them suffering," she said. We warmly approved of this admirable sentiment. But then, as she turned aside, she added quietly: "Unless, of course, they're sparrows."

A year or two ago the papers described a singular accident at a railway station, where a cow got on the line and was wedged between the platform and a moving train: the cow, we were told, was killed, "but fortunately there was no personal injury" — a view of the occurrence which seemed, to a humanitarian, still stranger than the accident itself.

Here, again, is an instance of unintended humour: "Homeward Bound" as the title of a cheerful picture in which a bronzed sailor is represented returning from the tropics, carrying — a caged parrot.

It is this traditional habit of regarding the lower animals not as persons and fellow-beings, but as automata and "things," that lies behind the determined refusal to recognize that they have rights, and is thus ultimately responsible for much of the callousness with which they are treated. With this superstition the League was in conflict from the first.

But perhaps some of my readers may still think that time spent on the rights of animals is so much taken away from the great human interests that are at stake. Let us help men first, they may argue, and then, when mankind is righted, we can help the animals after. On the other hand, there are some zoophilists who take the contrary view that men can help themselves, and that it is the animals first and foremost who need aid and protection. The League's opinion was that both these arguments are mistaken, and, for the same reason, viz. that, in our complex modern society, all great issues of justice or injustice are crossed and intermingled, so that no one cruelty can be singled out as the source of all other cruelties, nor can any one reform be fully realized apart from the rest. By "humanitarian" we meant one who feels and acts humanely, not towards mankind only, or the lower animals only, but towards all sentient life — one who adopts the Humanitarian League's principle that "it is iniquitous to inflict avoidable suffering on any sentient being." We did not regard as humanitarians, for example, those "philanthropic" persons who, having made a fortune by commercial competition, in which the depreciation of wages was a recognized method, afterwards gave back a portion of their wealth in "charity." This might, perhaps, be philanthropy, but it did not seem to be quite humanity. Nor did we think that the name "humanitarian" should be given to those zoophilists or animal lovers who keep useless and pampered animals as pets and playthings, wasting on them time and money which might be better spent elsewhere, and indeed wasting the lives of the animals themselves, for animals have their own lives to live as men have.

Perhaps the most able of all vindications of humane principles is that contained in Mr. Howard Moore's *The Universal Kinship*, published by the League in 1906. It was through a notice which I wrote in the *Humanitarian* of an earlier book of his, *Better-World Philosophy*, that the League first came into association with him; and I remember with shame that when that "sociological synthesis," as its sub-title proclaimed it to be, first came into my hands, I nearly left it unread, suspecting it to be but the latest of the many wearisome ethical treatises that are a scourge to the reviewer, to whom the very word "sociology" or "synthesis" is a terror. But fortunately I read the book, and quickly discovered its merits; and from that time, till his death in 1916, Howard Moore was one of the truest and tenderest of our friends, himself prone to despondency and, as his books show, with a touch of pessimism, yet never failing in his support and encouragement of others and of all humanitarian effort. "What on earth would we Unusuals do, in this lonely dream of life," so he wrote in one of his letters, "if it were not for the sympathy and friendship of the Few?"

Howard Moore died by his own hand (he had good reason for his action); and the timorous attitude which so many people adopt towards suicide was shown in the silence on this point which was maintained in most of the English zoophilist journals which mentioned his death: one editor hit upon the sagacious announcement that "he died very suddenly," which deserves, I think, to be noted as a consummate instance of how the truth may be truthfully obscured.

In *The Universal Kinship*, Howard Moore left to humanitarians a treasure which it will be their own fault if they do not value as it deserves. There is a tendency to forget that it is to modern evolutionary science that the ethic of humaneness owes its strongest corroboration. The physical basis of the humane philosophy rests on the biological fact that kinship is universal. Starting from this admitted truth, Moore showed, with much wealth of argument and epigram, that the supposed psychical gulf between human and non-human has no more existence, apart from the imagination of man, than the physical gulf which has now been bridged by science. The purpose of our movement was admirably stated by him: "to put science and humanitarianism in place of tradition and savagery." It was with that aim in view that our League of Humaneness had been formed.

*Seventy Years Among Savages*

## SALT AND ANIMALS' RIGHTS

### The Sending of the Animals

The Animals, you say, were "sent"
For man's free use and nutriment.
Pray, then, inform me, and be candid,
Why came they aeons before Man did,
To spend long centuries on earth,
Awaiting their Devourer's birth?
Those ill-timed chattels, sent from Heaven,
Were, sure, the maddest gift e'er given—
"Sent" for Man's usage (can Man believe it?)
When there was no Man to receive it!

*Cum Grano*

GRACE: I abominate Vivisection as the most horrible of crimes — the more horrble just because it is done, as Dr. Kersterman says, deliberately and conscientiously (we must grant him that), and not from mere thoughtlessness, like sport. But if we are to fight Vivisection, we must rid ourselves of this false "love of animals," this pampering of pets and lap-dogs by people who care nothing for the real welfare of animals, or even for the welfare of men. Humanitarianism must show that it is *not* "bestiarian," and must aim at the redress of *all* needless suffering, human and animal alike — the stupid cruelties of social tyranny, of the criminal code, of fashion, of science, of flesh-eating.

"A Lover of Animals," a play reprinted in Hendrick, *Henry Salt*

### A Lover of Animals

Oh, yes! you love them well, I know!
But whisper me — when most?
"In fields, at summer-time." Not so:
At supper-time — in roast.

*Cum Grano*

### The Principle of Animals' Rights

Have the lower animals "rights"? Undoubtedly — if men have. That is the point I wish to make evident in this opening chapter. But have men rights? Let it be stated at the outset that I have no intention of discussing the abstract theory of rights, which at the present time is looked upon with suspicion and disfavour by many social reformers, since it has not unfrequently been made to cover the most extravagant and contradictory assertions. But though its phraseology is vague, there is nevertheless a solid truth underlying it — a truth which has always been clearly apprehended by the moral faculty, however difficult it may be to establish it on an unassailable logical basis. If men have not "rights" — well, they have an unmistakable intimation of something very similar; a sense of justice which marks the boundary-line where

acquiescence ceases and resistance begins; a demand for freedom
to live their own lives, subject to the necessity of respecting the
equal freedom of other people.

Such is the doctrine of rights as formulated by Herbert Spencer.
"Every man," he says, "is free to do that which he wills, provided he infringes not the equal liberty of any other man." And
again, "Whoever admits that each man must have a certain
restricted freedom, asserts that it is *right* he should have this
restricted freedom. . . . And hence the several particular free-
doms deducible may fitly be called, as they commonly are called,
his *rights*" ("Justice," pp. 46, 62).[1]

The fitness of this nomenclature is disputed, but the existence
of some real principle of the kind can hardly be called in question;
so that the controversy concerning "rights" is little else than an
academic battle over words, which leads to no practical conclusion. I shall assume, therefore, that men are possessed of
"rights," in the sense of Herbert Spencer's definition; and if any
of my readers object to this qualified use of the term, I can only
say that I shall be perfectly willing to change the word as soon
as a more appropriate one is forthcoming.[2] The immediate question that claims our attention is this — if men have rights, have
animals their rights also?

From the earliest times there have been thinkers who, directly
or indirectly, answered this question with an affirmative. The
Buddhist and Pythagorean canons, dominated perhaps by the
creed of reincarnation, included the maxim "not to kill or injure
any innocent animal." The humanitarian philosophers of the
Roman empire, among whom Seneca, Plutarch, and Porphyry
were the most conspicuous, took still higher ground in preaching
humanity on the broadest principle of universal benevolence.

---

[1] An admirable definition of Rights is given by Mr. G. W. Foote in his contribu-
tion to "The New Charter": "Rights are of three sorts — legal, moral, and natural.
The legal meaning of 'Rights' is undoubtedly the primary one . . . and this is the
only *definite* sense in which the word can be used . . . Moral Rights are widespread
new sentiments, demanding incorporation into Legal Rights; and Natural Rights
are still newer sentiments, aspiring to recognition as Moral Rights, with a view
to ultimate incorporation as Legal Rights. . . . They are respectively, a solid fact,
a general demand, and a growing aspiration."

[2] This remark implies not the "disparagement of logic and of all careful use of
language," with which Professor D. G. Ritchie has charged me in his book on
"Natural Rights," but simply that social reformers cannot be debarred from using
the best available terms because no logically exact term is forthcoming.

"Since justice is due to rational beings," wrote Porphyry, "how is it possible to evade the admission that we are bound also to act justly towards the races below us?"

It is a lamentable fact that during the churchdom of the middle ages, from the fourth century to the sixteenth, from the time of Porphyry to the time of Montaigne, little or no attention was paid to the question of the rights and wrongs of the lower races. Then, with the Reformation and the revival of learning, came a revival also of humanitarian feeling, as may be seen in many passages of Erasmus and More, Shakespeare and Bacon; but it was not until the eighteenth century, the age of enlightenment and "sensibility," of which Voltaire and Rousseau were the spokesmen, that the rights of animals obtained more deliberate recognition. From the great Revolution of 1789 dates the period when the world-wide spirit of humanitarianism, which had hitherto been felt by but one man in a million — the thesis of the philosopher or the vision of the poet — began to disclose itself, gradually and dimly at first, as an essential feature of democracy.

A great and far-reaching effect was produced in England at this time by the publication of such revolutionary works as Thomas Paine's "Rights of Man" and Mary Wollstonecraft's "Vindication of the Rights of Women"; and looking back now, after the lapse of a hundred years, we can see that a still wider extension of the theory of rights was thenceforth inevitable. In fact, such a claim was anticipated — if only in bitter jest — by a contemporary writer, who furnishes us with a notable instance of how the mockery of one generation may become the reality of the next. There was published anonymously in 1792 a little volume entitled "A Vindication of the Rights of Brutes,"[1] a *reductio ad absurdum* of Mary Wollstonecraft's essay, written, as the author informs us, "to evince by demonstrative arguments the perfect equality of what is called the irrational species to the human." The further opinion is expressed that "after those wonderful productions of Mr. Paine and Mrs. Wollstonecraft, such a theory as the present seems to be necessary." It *was* necessary; and a very short term of years sufficed to bring it into effect; indeed, the theory had already been put forward by several English pioneers of nineteenth-century humanitarianism.

[1]Attributed to Thomas Taylor, the Platonist.

To Jeremy Bentham, in particular, belongs the high honour of first asserting the rights of animals with authority and persistence.

"The legislator," he wrote, "ought to interdict everything which may serve to lead to cruelty. The barbarous spectacles of gladiators no doubt contributed to give the Romans that ferocity which they displayed in their civil wars. A people accustomed to despise human life in their games could not be expected to respect it amid the fury of their passions. It is proper for the same reason to forbid every kind of cruelty towards animals, whether by way of amusement, or to gratify gluttony. Cock-fights, bull-baiting, hunting hares and foxes, fishing, and other amusements of the same kind, necessarily suppose either the absence of reflection or a fund of inhumanity, since they produce the most acute sufferings to sensible beings, and the most painful and lingering death of which we can form any idea. Why should the law refuse its protection to any sensitive being? The time will come when humanity will extend its mantle over everything which breathes. We have begun by attending to the condition of slaves; we shall finish by softening that of all the animals which assist our labours or supply our wants."[1]

So, too, wrote one of Bentham's contemporaries: "The grand source of the unmerited and superfluous misery of beasts exists in a defect in the constitution of all communities. No human government, I believe, has ever recognized the *jus animalium*, which ought surely to form a part of the jurisprudence of every system founded on the principles of justice and humanity."[2] A number of later moralists have followed on the same lines, with the result that the rights of animals have already, to a certain limited extent, been established both in private usage and by legal enactment.

It is interesting to note the exact commencement of this new princple in law. When Lord Erskine, speaking in the House of Lords in 1811, advocated the cause of justice to the lower animals, he was greeted with loud cries of insult and derision. But eleven years later the efforts of the despised humanitarians, and especially of Richard Martin, of Galway, were rewarded by their first success. The passing of the Ill-treatment of Cattle Bill, commonly known as "Martin's Act," in July, 1822, is a memorable date in

---

[1] "Principles of Penal Law," chap. xvi., 1780.
[2] John Lawrence, "Philosophical Treatise on the Moral Duties of Man towards the Brute Creation," 1796.

the history of humane legislation, less on account of the positive protection afforded by it, for it applied only to cattle and "beasts of burden," than for the invaluable precedent which it created. From 1822 onward, the principle of that *jus animalium* for which Bentham had pleaded, was recognized, however partially and tentatively at first, by English law, and the animals included in the Act ceased to be the mere property of their owners; moreover the Act has been several times supplemented and extended during the past half century. It is scarcely possible, in the face of this legislation, to maintain that "rights" are a privilege with which none but human beings can be invested; for if *some* animals are already included within the pale of protection, why should not more and more be so included in the future?[1]

For the present, however, what is most urgently needed is some comprehensive and intelligible principle, which shall indicate, in a more consistent manner, the true lines of man's moral relation towards the lower animals. Hitherto even the leading advocates of animals' rights seem to have shrunk from basing their claim on the only argument which can ultimately be held to be a sufficient one — the assertion that animals, as well as men, though, of course, to a far less extent than men, are possessed of a distinctive individuality, and therefore are in justice entitled to live their lives with a due measure of that "restricted freedom" to which Herbert Spencer alludes. It is of little use to claim "rights" for animals in a vague general way, if with the same breath we explicitly show our determination to subordinate those rights to anything and everything that can be construed into a human "want"; nor will it ever be possible to obtain full justice for the lower races so long as we continue to regard them as beings of a wholly different order, and to ignore the significance of their numberless points of kinship with mankind.

For example, it has been said by a well-known writer on the subject of humanity to animals[2] that "the life of a brute, having no moral purpose, can best be understood ethically as representing

[1]Professor Ritchie contends in his "Natural Rights" that domestic animals have *not* been granted rights in English law. "Because a work of art, or some ancient monument, is protected by law from injury, do we speak of the *rights* of pictures or stones?" But the distinction is obvious — works of art are protected only as *property*, domestic animals as *sentient beings*, whether owned or unowned.

[2]"Fraser," November, 1863; "The Rights of Man and the Claims of Brutes," by Frances Power Cobbe.

the sum of its *pleasures*; and the obligation, therefore, of producing the pleasures of sentient creatures must be reduced, in their case, to the abstinence from unnecessary destruction of life." Now, with respect to this statement, I must say that the notion of the life of an animal having "no moral purpose" belongs to a class of ideas which cannot possibly be accepted by the advanced humanitarian thought of the present day — it is a purely arbitrary assumption, at variance with our best science, and absolutely fatal (if the subject be clearly thought out) to any full realization of animals' rights. If we are ever going to do justice to the lower races, we must get rid of the antiquated notion of a "great gulf" fixed between them and mankind, and must recognize the common bond of humanity that unites all living beings in one universal brotherhood.

As far as any excuses can be alleged, in explanation of the insensibility or inhumanity of the western nations in their treatment of animals, these excuses may be mostly traced back to one or the other of two theories, wholly different in origin, yet alike in this — that both postulate an absolute difference of nature between men and the lower kinds.

The first is the so-called "religious" notion, which awards immortality to man, but to man alone, thereby furnishing (especially in Catholic countries) a quibbling justification for acts of cruelty to animals, on the plea that they "have no souls." "It should seem," says Mrs. Jameson,[1] "as if the primitive Christians, by laying so much stress upon a future life, in contradistinction to *this* life, and placing the lower creatures out of the pale of hope, placed them at the same time out of the pale of sympathy, and thus laid the foundation for this utter disregard of animals in the light of our fellow-creatures."

I am aware that a quite contrary argument has, in a few isolated instances, been founded on the belief that animals have "no souls." "Cruelty to a brute," says an old writer,[2] "is an injury irreparable," because there is no future life to be a compensation for present afflictions; and there is an amusing story, told by Mr. Lecky in his "History of European Morals," of a certain humanely-minded Cardinal, who used to allow vermin to bite him without hindrance, on the ground that *"we* shall have

[1] "Book of Thoughts, Memories, and Fancies," 1854.
[2] Humphrey Primatt, D.D., author of "The Duty of Mercy to Brute Animals" (1776).

heaven to reward us for our sufferings, but these poor creatures have nothing but the enjoyment of this present life." But this is a rare view of the question which need not, I think, be taken into very serious account; for, on the whole, the denial of immortality to animals (unless, of course, it be also denied to men) tends strongly to lessen their chance of being justly and considerately treated. Among the many humane movements of the present age, none is more significant than the growing inclination, noticeable both in scientific circles and in religious, to believe that mankind and the lower animals have the same destiny before them.[1]

The second and not less fruitul source of modern inhumanity is to be found in the "Cartesian" doctrine — the theory of Descartes and his followers — that the lower animals are devoid of consciousness and feeling; a theory which carried the "religious" notion a step further, and deprived the animals not only of their claim to a life hereafter, but of anything that could, without mockery, be called a life in the present, since mere "animated machines," as they were thus affirmed to be, could in no real sense be said to *live* at all! Well might Voltaire turn his humane ridicule against this most monstrous contention, and suggest, with scathing irony, that God "had given the animals the organs of feeling, to the end that they might *not* feel!" "The theory of animal automatism," says Professor Romanes, "which is usually attributed to Descartes, can never be accepted by common sense." Yet it is to be feared that it has done much, in its time, to harden "scientific" sense against the just complaints of the victims of human arrogance and oppression.[2]

Let me here quote a most impressive passage from Schopenhauer.

"The unpardonable forgetfulness in which the lower animals have hitherto been left by the moralists of Europe is well known. It is pretended that the beasts have no rights. They persuade themselves that our conduct in regard to them has nothing to do

[1]See the article on "Animal Immortality," "The Nineteenth Century," Jan., 1891, by Norman Pearson. The upshot of his argument is that, "if we accept the imortality of the human soul, and *also* accept its evolutional origin, we cannot deny the survival, in some form or other, of animal minds."

[2]Prof. Huxley's remarks, in "Science and Culture," give a partial support to Descartes' theory, but do not bear on the moral question of rights. For, though he concludes that animals are probably "sensitive automata," he classes men in the same category.

with morals, or (to speak the language of their morality) that we have no duties towards animals: a doctrine revolting, gross, and barbarous, peculiar to the west, and having its root in Judaism. In philosophy, however, it is made to rest upon a hypothesis, admitted in despite of evidence itself, of an absolute difference between man and beast. It is Descartes who has proclaimed it in the clearest and most decisive manner; and in fact it was a necessary consequence of his errors. The Cartesian-Leibnitzian-Wolfian philosophy, with the assistance of entirely abstract notions, had built up the 'rational psychology,' and constructed an immortal *anima rationalis*: but, visibly, the world of beasts, with its very natural claims, stood up against this exclusive monopoly — this *brevet* of immortality decreed to man alone — and silently Nature did what she always does in such cases — she protested. Our philosophers, feeling their scientific conscience quite disturbed, were forced to attempt to consolidate their 'rational psychology' by the aid of empiricism. They therefore set themselves to work to hollow out between man and beast an enormous abyss, of an immeasurable width; by this they wish to prove to us, in contempt of evidence, an impassable difference."[1]

The fallacious idea that the lives of animals have no moral purpose is at root connected with these religious and philosophical pretensions which Schopenhauer so powerfully condemns. To live one's own life — to realize one's true self — is the highest moral purpose of man and animal alike; and that animals possess their due measure of this sense of individuality is scarcely open to doubt. "We have seen," says Darwin, "that the senses and intuitions, the various emotions and faculties, such as love, memory, attention, curiosity, imitation, reason, etc., of which man boasts, may be found in an incipient, or even sometimes in a well-developed condition, in the lower animals."[2] Not less emphatic is the testimony of the Rev. J. G. Wood, who, speaking from a great experience, gives it as his opinion that "the manner in which we ignore individuality in the lower animals is simply astounding." He claims for them a future life, because he is "quite sure that most of the cruelties which are perpetrated on the animals are due to the habit of considering them as mere

---

[1]Schopenhauer's "Foundation of Morality." I quote the passage as translated in Mr. Howard Williams's "Ethics of Diet."
[2]"Descent of Man," chap. iii.

machines without susceptibilities, without reason, and without the capacity of a future."[1]

The long-maintained distinction between human "reason" and animal "instinct" is being given up by recent scientific writers, as, for example, by Dr. Wesley Mills in his work on "The Nature and Development of Animal Intelligence," and by Mr. E. P. Evans in "Evolutional Ethics and Animal Psychology."

> "The trend of investigation," says Dr. Mills, "thus far goes to show that at least the germ of every human faculty does exist in some species of animal. . . . Formerly the line was drawn at reason. It was said that the 'brutes' cannot reason. Only persons who do not themselves reason about the subject with the facts before them can any longer occupy such a position. The evidence of reasoning power is overwhelming for the upper ranks of animals, and yearly the downward limits are being extended the more the inferior tribes are studied."

We have to get rid, as Mr. Evans points out, of those "anthropocentric" delusions which "treat man as a being essentially different and inseparably set apart from all other sentient creatures, to which he is bound by no ties of mental affinity or moral obligation."

> "Man is as truly a part and product of Nature as any other animal, and this attempt to set him up as an isolated point outside of it is philosophically false and morally pernicious."

This, then, is the position of those who assert that animals, like men, are possessed of certain limited rights, which cannot be withheld from them, as they are now withheld, without tyranny and injustice. They have individuality, character, reason; and to have those qualities is to have the right to exercise them, in so far as surrounding circumstances permit. No human being is justified in regarding an animal as a meaningless automaton, to be worked, or tortured, or eaten, as the case may be, for the mere object of satisfying the wants or whims of mankind. Together with the destinies and duties that are laid on them and fulfilled by them, animals have also the right to be treated with gentleness and consideration, and the man who does not so treat them, however great his learning or influence may be, is, in that respect, an ignorant and foolish man, devoid of the highest and noblest culture of which the human mind is capable.

[1] "Man and Beast, here and hereafter," 1874.

Something must here be said on the important subject of nomenclature. It is to be feared that the ill-treatment of animals is largely caused — or at any rate the difficulty of amending that treatment is largely aggravated — by the common use of such terms as "brute-beast," "live-stock," etc., which implicitly deny to the lower races that intelligent individuality which is undoubtedly possessed by them. It was long ago remarked by Bentham, in his "Introduction to Principles of Morals and Legislation," that, whereas human beings are styled *persons*, "other animals, on account of their interests having been neglected by the insensibility of the ancient jurists, stand degraded into the class of *things*"; and Schopenhauer also has commented on the mischievous absurdity of the idiom which applies the neuter pronoun "it" to such highly organized animals as the dog and the ape.

A word of protest is needed also against such an expression as "dumb animals," which, though often cited as "an immense exhortation to pity,"[1] has in reality a tendency to influence ordinary people in quite the contrary direction, inasmuch as it fosters the idea of an impassable barrier between mankind and their dependents. It is convenient to us men to be deaf to the entreaties of the victims of our injustice; and, by a sort of grim irony, we therefore assume that it is *they* who are afflicted by some organic incapacity — they are "dumb animals," forsooth! Although a moment's consideration must prove that they have innumerable ways, often quite human in variety and suggestiveness, of uttering their thoughts and emotions. Even the term "animals," as applied to the lower races, is incorrect, and not wholly unobjectionable, since it ignores the fact that *man* is an animal no less than they. My only excuse for using it in this volume is that there is no better brief term available.

So anomalous is the attitude of man towards the lower animals, that it is no marvel if many humane thinkers have wellnigh despaired over this question. "The whole subject of the brute creation," wrote Dr. Arnold, "is to me one of such painful mystery, that I dare not approach it"; and this (to put the most

---

[1] In Sir A. Helps's "Animals and their Masters." See an article on "Dumb Animals," in "The Humanitarian," November, 1912. Also the chapter on "Speech as a Barrier between Man and Beast," in Mr. E. P. Evans's work on "Evolutional Ethics and Animal Psychology," 1898.

charitable interpretation on their silence) appears to be the position of the majority of moralists and teachers at the present time. Yet there is urgent need of some solution of the problem; and in no other way can this be found than by the admission of the lower races within the pale of human sympathy. All the promptings of our best and surest instincts point us in this direction. "It is abundantly evident," says Lecky, "both from history and from present experience, that the instinctive shock, or natural feelings of disgust, caused by the sight of the sufferings of men, is not generically different from that which is caused by the sight of the suffering of animals." If this be so, can it be seriously contended that the same humanitarian tendency which has already emancipated the slave, will not ultimately benefit the lower races also? Here, again, the historian of "European Morals" has a significant remark:

> "At one time the benevolent affections embrace merely the family, soon the circle expanding includes first a class, then a nation, then a coalition of nations, then all humanity; and finally its influence is felt in the dealings of man with the animal world. In each of these cases a standard is formed, different from that of the preceding stage, but in each case the same tendency is recognized as virtue."

But, it may be argued, vague sympathy with the lower animals is one thing, and a definite recognition of their "rights" is another; what reason is there to suppose that we shall advance from the former phase to the latter? Just this; that every great liberating movement has proceeded exactly on such lines. Oppression and cruelty are invariably founded on a lack of imaginative sympathy; the tyrant or tormentor can have no true sense of kinship with the victim of his injustice. When once the sense of affinity is awakened, the knell of tyranny is sounded, and the ultimate concession of "rights" is simply a matter of time. The present condition of the more highly organized domestic animals is in many ways very analogous to that of the negro slaves of a hundred years ago: look back, and you will find in their case precisely the same exclusion from the common pale of humanity; the same hypocritical fallacies, to justify that exclusion; and, as a consequence, the same deliberate stubborn denial of their social "rights." Look back — for it is well to do so — and then look forward, and the moral can hardly be mistaken.

We find so great a thinker as Aristotle seriously pondering, in his "Ethics," whether a slave may be considered as a fellow-being. In emphasizing the point that friendship is founded on propinquity, he expresses himself as follows:

> "Neither can men have friendships with horses, cattle, or slaves, considered merely as such; for a slave is merely a living instrument, and an instrument a lifeless slave. Yet, considered as a man, a slave may be an object of friendship, for certain rights seem to belong to all those capable of participating in law and engagement."

Slaves, says Bentham,

> "have been treated by the law exactly upon the same footing as in England, for example, the inferior races of animals are still. The day may come when the rest of the animal creation may acquire those rights which could never have been withholden from them but by the hand of tyranny."

Let us unreservedly admit the immense difficulties that stand in the way of this animal enfranchisement. Our relation towards the animals is complicated and embittered by innumerable habits handed down through centuries of brutality and mistrust; we cannot, in all cases, suddenly relax these habits, or do full justice even where we see that justice will have to be done. A perfect ethic of humaneness is therefore impracticable, if not unthinkable; and we can attempt to do no more than to indicate in a general way the main principle of animals' rights, noting at the same time the most flagrant particular violations of those rights, and the lines on which the only valid reform can hereafter be effected. But, on the other hand, it may be remembered, for the comfort and encouragement of humanitarian workers, that these obstacles are, after all, only such as are inevitable in each branch of social improvement; for at every stage of every great reformation it has been repeatedly argued, by indifferent or hostile observers, that further progress is impossible; indeed, when the opponents of a great cause begin to demonstrate its "impossibility," experience teaches us that that cause is already on the high road to fulfilment.

As for the demand so frequently made on reformers, that they should first explain the details of their scheme — how this and that point will be arranged, and by what process all kinds of difficulties, real or imagined, will be circumvented — the only rational reply is that it is absurd to expect to see the end of a question when we are now but at its beginning. The persons who offer this futile sort of criticism are usually those who under no circumstances would be open to conviction; they purposely ask for an explanation which, by the very nature of the case, is impossible because it necessarily belongs to a later period of time. It would be equally sensible to request a traveller to enumerate beforehand all the particular things he will see by the way, on pain of being denounced as an unpractical visionary, although he may have a quite sufficient general knowledge of his course and destination.

Our main principle is now clear. If "rights" exist at all — and both feeling and usage indubitably prove that they do exist — they cannot be consistently awarded to men and denied to animals, since the same sense of justice and compassion apply in both cases. "Pain is pain," says Humphrey Primatt, "whether it be inflicted on man or on beast; and the creature that suffers it, whether man or beast, being sensible of the misery of it while it lasts, suffers *evil*; and the sufferance of evil, unmeritedly, unprovokedly, where no offence has been given, and no good can possibly be answered by it, but merely to exhibit power or gratify malice, is Cruelty and Injustice in him that occasions it."

I commend this outspoken utterance to the attention of those ingenious moralists who quibble about the "discipline" of suffering, and deprecate immediate attempts to redress what, it is alleged, may be a necessary instrument for the attainment of human welfare. It is perhaps a mere coincidence, but it may be observed that those who are most forward to disallow the rights of others, and to argue that suffering and subjection are the natural lot of all living things, are usually themselves exempt from the operation of this beneficent law, and that the beauty of self-sacrifice is most loudly belauded by those who profit most largely at the expense of their fellow-beings.

But "nature is one with rapine," say some, and this utopian theory of "rights," if too widely extended, must come in conflict with that iron rule of internecine competition by which the universe is regulated. But is the universe so regulated? We note that this very objection, which was confidently relied on a few years back by many opponents of the emancipation of the working-classes, is not heard of in that connection now. Our learned economists and men of science, who set themselves to play the defenders of the social *status quo*, have seen their own weapons of "natural selection," "survival of the fittest," and what not, snatched from their hands and turned against them, and are therefore beginning to explain to us, in a scientific manner, what we untutored humanitarians had previously felt to be true, viz., that competition is not by any means the sole governing law among the human race. We are not greatly dismayed, then, to find the same old bugbear trotted out as an argument against animals' rights — indeed, we see already unmistakable signs of a similar reversal of the scientific judgment.[1]

The charge of "sentimentalism" is frequently brought against those who plead for animals' rights. Now "sentimentalism," if any meaning at all can be attached to the word, must signify an inequality, an ill balance of sentiment, an inconsistency which leads men into attacking one abuse, while they ignore or condone another where a reform is equally desirable. That this weakness is often observable among "philanthropists" on the one hand, and "friends of animals" on the other, and most of all among those acute "men of the world," whose regard is only for themselves, I am not concerned to deny; what I wish to point out is, that the only real safeguard against sentimentality is to take up a consistent position towards the rights of men and of the lower animals alike, and to cultivate a broad sense of universal justice (not "mercy") for all living things. Herein, and herein alone, is to be sought the true sanity of temperament.

It is an entire mistake to suppose that the rights of animals are in any way antagonistic to the rights of men. Let us not be betrayed for a moment into the specious fallacy that we must study human rights first, and leave the animal question to solve itself hereafter; for it is only by a wide and disinterested study of *both* subjects that a solution of either is possible. "For he who loves all animated nature," says Porphyry, "will not hate any

[1]See Prince Kropotkin's articles on "Mutual Aid among Animals," "Nineteenth Century," 1890, where the conclusion is arrived at that "sociability is as much a law of nature as mutual struggle." A similar view is expressed in the "Study of Animal Life," 1892, by J. Arthur Thomson. "What we must protest against," he says, in an interesting chapter on "The Struggle of Life," "is that one-sided interpretation according to which individualistic competition is nature's sole method of progress.'

Another and more recent work, which has a very important bearing on this question, is "Symbiosis: a Socio-Physiological Study of Evolution," by H. Reinheimer, 1920.

one tribe of innocent beings, and by how much greater his love for the whole, by so much the more will he cultivate justice towards a part of them, and that part to which he is most allied." To omit all worthier reasons, it is too late in the day to suggest the indefinite postponement of a consideration of animals' rights, for from a moral point of view, and even from a legislative point of view, we are daily confronted with the problem, and the so-called "practical" people who affect to ignore it are simply shutting their eyes to facts which they find it disagreeable to confront.

Once more then, animals have rights, and these rights consist in the "restricted freedom" to live a natural life — a life, that is, which permits of the individual development — subject to the limitations imposed by the permanent needs and interests of the community. There is nothing quixotic or visionary in this assertion; it is perfectly compatible with a readiness to look the sternest laws of existence fully and honestly in the face. If we must kill, whether it be man or animal, let us kill and have done with it; if we must inflict pain, let us do what is inevitable, without hypocrisy, or evasion, or cant. But (here is the cardinal point) let us first be assured that it *is* necessary; let us not wantonly trade on the needless miseries of other beings, and then attempt to lull our consciences by a series of shuffling excuses which cannot endure a moment's candid investigation. As Leigh Hunt well says:

> "That there is pain and evil, is no rule
> That I should make it greater, like a fool."

Thus far the general principle of animals' rights . . .

*Animals' Rights*


That particular form of recreation which is euphemistically known as "sport" has a close historical connection with the practice of flesh-eating, inasmuch as the hunter was in old times what the butcher is now, — the "purveyor" on whom the family was dependent for its daily supply of victuals. Modern sport, however, as usually carried on in civilized European countries, has degenerated into what as been well described as "amateur butchery," a system under which the slaughter of certain kinds of animals is practised less as a necessity than as a means of amusement and diversion. Just as the youthful nobles, during the savage scenes and reprisals of the Huguenot wars, used to seize the opportunity of exercising their swordsmanship, and perfecting themselves in the art of dealing graceful death-blows, so the modern sportsman converts the killing of animals from a prosaic and perhaps distasteful business into an agreeable and gentlemanly pastime.

\* \* \*

It is idle to spend a single moment in advocating the rights of the lower animals, if such rights do not include a total and un-qualified exemption from the awful tortures of vivisection — from the doom of being slowly and mercilessly dismembered, or flayed, or baked alive, or infected with some deadly virus, or subjected to any of the numerous modes of torture inflicted by the Scientific Inquisition.

\* \* \*

The terrible sufferings that are quite needlessly inflicted on the lower animals under the plea of domestic usage, food-demands, sport, fashion, and science, are patent to all who have the seeing eye and the feeling heart to apprehend them; those sufferings will not be lessened, nor will man's responsibility be diminished by any such irrelevant assertions as that vivisection is less cruel than sport, or sport less cruel than butchering, — nor yet by the contrary contention that vivisection, or sport, or flesh-eating, as the case may be, is the prime origin of all human inhumanity. We want a comprehensive principle which will cover all these varying instances, and determine the true lines of reform.

Such a principle, as I have throughout insisted, can only be found in the recognition of the right of animals, as of men, to be exempt from any unnecessary suffering or serfdom, the right to live a natural life of "restricted freedom," subject to the real, not supposed or pretended, requirements of the general community.

From *Animals' Rights*

### *"He" and "It"*

("Strange fact, that the English language makes all
animals of the neuter gender."—SCHOPENHAUER)

"He" was a man, a worthless wight,
　　Who drank, and knew no shame,
Till, reckless, on some frenzied night,
　　He set his house aflame.

"It" was a dog that instant ran,
　　By faithful love made brave;
How base soe'er might be the man,
　　A master's life to save.

"A gallant dog!" the neighbours cried,
　　And praised such canine wit;
Then, wondering, spread the story wide
　　How "he" was saved by "it"!

*Cum Grano*

### *Mr. Facing-Both-Ways*

When the Huntsman claims praise for the
　　killing of foxes,
Who else would bring ruin to farmer and land,
Yet so kindly imports them, preserves them,
　　assorts them—
There's a discrepance here that I'd fain understand.

When the Butcher makes boast of the killing
　　of cattle,
That would multiply fast and the world over-run,
Yet so carefully breeds them, rears, fattens, and
　　feeds them—
Here also, methinks, a fine cobweb is spun.

Hark you, then, whose profession or pastime is
　　killing!
To dispel your benignant illusion I'm loth:
But be one or the other, my double-faced brother,
Be Slayer or Saviour—you cannot be both.

*Cum Grano*

## SALT ON TORTURES

### The Hymn of the Flagellomaniacs

As the miser craves for treasure
   As the drunkard craves for grog,
So we crave for morbid pleasure—
   Something sentient to flog!

Give us juvenile offender,
   Truant oft from school or church,
Yet for prison cell too tender:—
   Ah! to brand him with the birch!

Give us gaol-bird past repentance,
   Brutalised too deep for that:—
Ah! to wreak on him the sentence
   Of the sanguinary 'cat'!

All the tortures—hanging, burning,
   Cropping, thumbscrew, boot, and rack—
Pale before our fevered yearning
   For the bare and bleeding back.

As the miser o'er his treasure.
   As the drunkard o'er his grog,
So we gloat with maniac pleasure
   O'er our joy of joys—to flog!

*Consolations of a Faddist*

[Suddenly, from a remote part of the prison, a prolonged, agonizing toneless screech is heard, followed by a complete hush]. . . .

B. 20. . . . It was the most horrible heart-shaking sound I ever heard in my life. What on earth was it, man? For God's sake, tell me.

Warder (grinning). It's the tune as you'll be singing yourself, B. 20, if you don't mend your manners. That's how they generally sing, when they get two dozen with the cat.

From "The Home Secretary's Holiday,"
a one-act play reproduced in Hendrick's *Henry Salt*

## Twentieth-Century Tortures

Why not bring back at once the boot, the stake, and the thumbscrew?—PROFESSOR LAWSON TAIT.

It is among the proudest boasts of this country that torture is not permitted within its borders: "Torture," wrote Macaulay, "was inflicted for the last time in the month of May, 1640." But pleasant though it is to think that it was in the beautiful springtime that the barbarous practice came to an end, this is unfortunately one of the cases in which our people allow themselves to be beguiled and fooled by very transparent quibbles; for a few minutes' thought would suffice to convince the most complacent of Britons that while some specialized forms of judicial torture have been abandoned, other tortures, some of them not less painful and fully as repulsive, are being inflicted to this day — nearly three hundred years after the glorious date of abolition. For if "torture," as etymology and the dictionaries and common usage tell us, means nothing more or less than the forcible infliction of extreme pain, it is not a technicality but an absurdity to pretend that it finds no place among twentieth-century institutions.

Flogging is torture in a most literal sense, and in one of its grossest shapes: the "cat," as Mr. G. K. Chesterton has well said, is "the rack without any of its intellectual reasons."[1] The horror of the old naval and military lashings is within the memory of many officers who were compelled to witness them: how is the punishment any less savage in its nature because it is now

[1]*Daily News*, June 6, 1908

administered in a less severe degree, and on men convicted of robbery with violence or some breach of prison discipline? In one of the Parliamentary debates of November, 1912, a Member who had been invited by the Home Secretary to examine the "cat," gave it as his opinion that "if *that* is not torture, then I do not know what torture is."

In the gloomiest but most impressive of his stories, *The Island of Dr. Moreau*, Mr. H. G. Wells has represented his savage "beastfolk" as monotonously chanting a certain "idiotic formula" about the infallibility of "the Law." With nothing more fitly than with this can be compared the undying legend, now over half a century old, that "garrotting was put down by the lash." It is not often that a popular fallacy, however erroneous it may be, can be actually disproved; but in this particular case such refutation was possible, in the certified fact that the garrotting "epidemic" of 1862 had been suppressed by the ordinary law *before* flogging for that offence was legalized. For many years the Humanitarian League issued a public challenge on the subject, and made the facts known in thousands of press letters; the challenge was quietly ignored, and the false statement repeated, till it was plain that, as De Quincey remarked, "rarer than the phoenix is that virtuous man who will consent to lose a prosperous story on the consideration that it happens to be a lie." One such virtuous man, however, and one only, was found, namely, Mr. Montague Crackanthorpe, who actually recanted the statement which he could not substantiate.[1] In view of his unique candour, it was suggested after his death that a statue should be erected to his memory.

Very different from the course taken by Mr. Crackanthorpe was the action of Sir Alexander Wood Renton, of the Supreme Court of Ceylon, who, in an article on "Corporal Punishment," introduced into the *Encyclopaedia Britannica* of 1910 that very garrotting legend from which it had previously been kept free, and made the further mistake of giving the date of the Flogging Act of 1863 as 1861, thus lending to his blunder a misleading appearance of plausibility. When called to account, he was content to maintain a masterly silence — more eloquent than words — and to allow his misstatement, unacknowledged and uncorrected, to continue to keep alive a prevalent superstition. Can it be wondered that

[1] *The Times*, December 11 and 26, 1902.

such fallacies persist, when a Chief Justice will thus lie low rather than admit himself at fault?

It is an amusing fact, and far too little known, that the text which has long lent a sanctity to the use of corporal punishment, is not taken, as supposed, from the *Proverbs* of Solomon, but from a passage, and a rather unseemly one, in Butler's *Hudibras* (1663):[1] this, however, is as it should be, for it is fitting that an indecent practice should claim authority from an indecent source. Thus encouraged, and with this divine precept in their thoughts, parents and schoolmasters, and magistrates, and judges, and all governors and rulers, have felt that in wielding the rod they were discharging a religious obligation, and not, as might otherwise have been suspected, gratifying some very primitive instincts of their own. For "the Wisdom of Solomon" has been quoted as our guide, in the correction of the old as well as of the young; indeed, as a writer in the *People* sagely remarked, "the older the evil-doer, the more his need of the birch." On this principle, aged vagrants have on various occasions been sentenced to be corrected with the rod; but it is to the young that the blessings of the birch more properly belong.

> Our British boys, from shore to shore,
> Two priceless boons may find:
> The Flag that's ever waved before,
> The Birch that's waved behind.

In its campaign against flogging in the Royal Navy, the Humanitarian League gained not only a considerable success, but an amount of entertainment which of itself would have more than repaid the labour expended on the work. To begin with, there was the technical quibble, very characteristic of officialdom, that though the backs of boys, or rather of young men, might be cut into ribbons with the birch, there was no "flogging" in the Navy, for "flogging" meant the infliction not of the birch but of the "cat." With Mr. Swift MacNeill conducting the attack in the House of Commons, it may be imagined that such prevarications — and there were many similar instances — fared but badly; and it was no surprise when "these degrading practices," as Sir Henry Campbell-Bannerman described them, were brought to an end in 1906, though the use of the cane, to the discredit of the Admiralty, is still permitted and defended.

[1] Then spare the rod and spoil the child.—*Hudibras*, Part II, canto 1, 844.

In this long controversy the League was brought into conflict with all sorts of opponents, among them several Admirals, of whom the "breeziest" were the Hon. V. A. Montagu and Sir William Kennedy. With the latter especially we had great fun, as we found in him an 'antagonist of the utmost heartiness and good humour. "Of what use is it," he wrote to me, "sending me all this rubbish, except to fill the waste-paper basket? I don't care a damn for Admiral ——'s opinion." On another occasion he sent me a formal challenge to meet him "at any time and place, when pistols and coffee will be provided." At a later date we had his support, equally emphatic, in our protest against the practice of feeding snakes on live prey at the "Zoo."

Other friends, too, helped to lend gaiety to a rather dismal subject. Among those who actively co-operated with the League was a commercial traveller, who was deeply versed in the various laws relating to corporal punishment, and who, as he once confided to me, had been in the habit of working locally as a sort of freelance and Bashi-Bazouk. He had made a practice, for example, of writing "How about the Birch?" on the Admiralty's printed notices in which boys were invited to reap the benefits of joining the Navy; and this had touched so sore a point that the advertisements in question had at length been put within glass frames. Another of his little jokes was to write to private schoolmasters, saying that he had a son whom he was about to send to school (which was true), and asking whether they could guarantee that there would be no corporal punishment. Several masters responded favourably, but as the boy could not be sent to more than one place of education, these worthy folk were deprived of their *quid pro quo*; in the end, however, a nemesis fell upon their betrayer, for once, when he had just returned home after a long journey, tired, and wanting above everything his tea, who should be announced but one of those very pedagogues with whom he had been in communication. He too had travelled some distance, rather than miss the chance of a pupil, and, having "ideas" on the subject of corporal punishment, had come, as he said, for "a good talk." "I could have eaten him," was our friend's remark.

In the 'nineties of the last century, the state of the Criminal Law, as Mr. Justice Mathew pointed out, was a hundred years behind the times, and a special department of the Humanitarian League was established in order to advocate certain much-needed reforms. It was felt that in view of the severity of the penal laws, the inequality of sentences, and the hard and indiscriminating character of prison discipline, an organized attempt ought to be made to humanize both the spirit of the law and the conditions of prison life, and to show that the true purpose of imprisonment was the reformation, not the mere punishment, of the offender. In this campaign the League was able to avail itself of a mass of expert information. It published, in 1893, a very effective pamphlet, "I was in Prison," written by Mr. Robert Johnson, director of the Colonial College at Hollesley Bay; and this was followed, a year later, by "A Plea for Mercy to Offenders," an address given before the League by Mr. C. H. Hopwood, the Recorder of Liverpool, who, with his friend Mr. Johnson, did great service in showing the futility of long sentences of imprisonment. I had several talks about that time with Mr. Johnson and Mr. Hopwood; and they would have thrown in their lot altogether with the Humanitarian League but for their fear that the inclusion within its programme of many other questions, such as sport and vivisection, would alienate sympathy in some quarters from their special subject of prison reform: it was for this reason that Mr. Hopwood afterwards founded the Romilly Society.

Two other names stood out conspicuously in the same sphere of work — that of Dr. W. Douglas Morrison, the well-known criminologist, now Rector of Marylebone, under whose guidance the League took a prominent part in the agitation which led to the Prisons Act of 1898, and that of "Lex," one of the keenest intellects of his time, whose pen was placed unreservedly at the League's disposal. Mr. W. H. S. Monck — for it was he who adopted that *nom de plume* — was Chief Registrar in Bankruptcy in the King's Bench Division, Dublin, a post which he filled with distinction, while his extraordinarily active and versatile mind found interest in many other studies: he was a mathematician, an astronomer, a writer on logic, political economy, and moral philosophy, and withal a chess-player of note, among which pursuits he never failed to find time to help the humanitarian cause. His official position made it desirable that his name should not appear; but many were the press letters that he wrote and many the resolutions, memorials, and letters to governmental departments that he drafted on the League's behalf. To "ask 'Lex' to draft it" was often the course taken by the Committee when dealing with some technical matter that needed exceptional care. The two subjects in which Mr. Monck was specially concerned, besides that of flogging, were the establishment of a Court of Criminal Appeal and a revision of the law relating to Imprisonment for Debt; and it was largely his unacknowledged labours that brought about the one reform and prepared the way for the other. In his press letters on corporal punishment he would sometimes adopt the ironic manner; that is, he would write as one who in part believed in the value of flogging, yet in such a way as to suggest rather the flaws and failures of the practice, and so to impair any faith in it which might linger in the minds of his readers.

Among other friends to whom this department of the League was much indebted were Mr. George Ives, author of *A History of Penal Methods*; Mrs. H. Bradlaugh Bonner; Mr. Carl Heath; Mr. H. B. Montgomery; Mrs. L. T. Mallet; Dr. T. Baty, the distinguished authority on International Law; and Mr. Joseph Collinson, who for some years acted as its honorary secretary. Mr. Collinson was a young north-countryman, self-taught, and full of native readiness and ingenuity, who at an early age had developed a passion for humanitarian journalism, and whose press letters became as well known as those of Mr. Algernon Ashton, while he had a marked advantage over that gentleman in having an ethical purpose and something definite to write about. Any one who should glance over the files of the chief London and provincial journals, between the years 1895 and 1910, could not fail to see a number of letters signed "Joseph Collinson," or to admire the pertinacity with which the humanitarian view of a host of controversial subjects, in particular those relating to criminal law and prisons, was brought to the notice of the public. Especially in regard to the flogging question Mr. Collinson's services were of great value.

Thus supported, the Humanitarian League had no cause to fear any reasoned opposition: our difficulty, rather, was to meet with any; for our antagonists were mostly anonymous and often abusive correspondents of newspapers, and the real obstacle with which we had to cope was the crass weight of prejudice and the immense stability of old institutions. Two of our adversaries, however, must not go without mention. One was Mr. William Tallack, then Secretary of the Howard Association, whose hostility was dangerous because it lurked under the guise of philanthropy. He was an old gentleman of benevolent demeanour, whose method it was to sit astutely "on the fence," making oracular utterances, now on that side, now on this, so that, like the writer of an astrological almanack, he might be able in any event to run in and cry: "I told you so." In his *Penological Principles*, a work much advertised in those days, there was plenty of penology, but very little principle, much more of the Tallack than of the Howard: it was, in fact, a farrago of platitudes and pieties, which said many things without ultimately meaning anything at all. Yet, in spite of his much verbiage and many estimable sentiments, Mr. Tallack was a reactionist; he belonged to an antiquated school of thought, quite out of sympathy with the new style of prison reform; and as he lost no opportunity of disparaging the work of the League, we showed him somewhat emphatically that that was a game at which two parties could play. This he did not relish, especially as we were strongly backed up by Mr. Passmore Edwards in his paper, the *Echo*. A conference was accordingly proposed by Mr. Tallack, where it was agreed that in future there should be a friendly arrangement of "hands off" on either side. I remember how, at that meeting, he told me in his paternal manner, as an instance of the advantages of not advocating "extreme" measures of reform, that he enjoyed the privilege of being able, now and then, to have a personal talk with the Home Secretary. "What would humanitarians think of that?" The old gentleman was evidently unaware that if he was a *persona grata* at the Home Office, it was precisely because he was known to be a "tame" reformer, a parasite of the old system, not a champion of the new, and therefore useful to those who wished to let matters go on as before.

In a prison-play "The Home Secretary's Holiday," which was acted before the Humanitarian League at one of its social gatherings, Mr. Tallack was glanced at in the character of Mr. Prim, a Visiting Justice, who dwells on the value of "segregation," "introspection," "self-questioning," and "remorse," as heaven-sent means by which the convicted sinner may be awakened to a sense of his guilt.

Our other critic, of whom I must say a brief word, was Sir Robert Anderson, then an ex-Assistant Commissioner of Police; who, being of a choleric and over-bearing nature, was consumed with wrathful indignation at the activities of the Humanitarian League. In his book on *Criminals and Crime*, vengeful tirades against the professional criminal were accompanied with scarcely less violent abuse of "professional humanitarians" — a strange term this, to be applied to honorary workers in an unpopular cause, and by one who had himself been for many years a salaried official at Scotland Yard! In the same work we figured variously at "humanity-mongers," "agitators," "fools," "hysterical faddists," "doctrinaire philanthropists," "spurious philosophers," "maudlin sentimentalists," and so on. Authors sometimes describe their books as "a labour of love." Sir Robert's was certainly a labour of hate, and among the punishments which he indicated as suitable for an impenitent thief were the gallows, crucifixion, thumb-screws, and the rack; he added that it was consideration for the community, not for the thief, that prevented the use of them. It is not pleasant to have to speak of such a man; one would rather forget him. But in estimating the savagery of the age, the fact that his most vindictive proposals met with a good deal of public support is one which cannot be left out of account.

A thorough-going condemnation of flogging is without doubt a very unpopular policy; the Humanitarian League lost many members and much pecuniary support by its steadfastness on this point, especially, strange to say, among zoophilists and anti-vivisectionists, many of whom were firm believers in the propriety of vivisecting the backs of criminals, and would have gone any distance, as I have heard said, "to see a vivisector flogged." Not the least valuable part of the League's duties was to put a check on foolish talk of that sort; and in this we had the satisfaction of being warmly supported by so distinguished an opponent of vivisection as Professor Lawson Tait. It came about in a rather strange way.

The League held a meeting in Birmingham; and a local member, who had the arrangements in hand, got Mr. Tait to preside, but by some oversight did not sufficiently apprise him beforehand of our aims and objects. When he entered the room — a formidable-looking figure, with slow gait, massive build, and heavy brows — he was seen to be in a towering rage. The storm broke at once. Instead of the usual complimentary remarks from the chair, he told us in wrathful tones that he knew nothing of the Humanitarian League, and that it was most improper that he should have been left thus uninformed. This was true, and we wished the earth would swallow us up; but there was nothing for it but to go on with the business of the meeting, and while the speeches were being made Mr. Tait sat and studied the League's printed manifesto. As he read it, the gloom gradually left him; he began to mutter approval of point after point, then to chuckle with satisfaction, and presently he turned to me (I happened to be sitting next to him) and told me that he was in complete agreement with our programme. A great good humour now took the place of his former resentment, and presently he spoke at some length, and himself moved a resolution that the objects of the League were "worthy the support of all good citizens." He declared that he felt almost as strongly on the question of prison punishments as on that of vivisection, and severely censured the clamour for the lash that had been raised by some woman-suffragists of Edinburgh. It was then that he used the words prefixed to this chapter: "Why not bring back at once the boot, the stake, and the thumbscrew?"

That there are numbers of persons who would be quite willing to bring back, if it were possible, the medieval forms of torture cannot for a moment be doubted by any one who, like myself, has had the experience of working for over twenty-five years for the discontinuance of flogging. There are, of course, many reasonable advocates of corporal punishment in one or another of its forms; but there are many more to whom the cry for flogging, and for more and yet more flogging, has become a veritable craze, as was seen when, in the agitation for the lashing of "white slavers" in 1912, a frenzied shriek of passion went up from a large section of the people. "We know," said a Member of Parliament at the time, "the extraordinary hysterical emotion which this Bill has aroused throughout England. We get letters from all sorts of people, chiefly women, 'flog them,' 'crucify them,' and anything else you like. It is a cry we have had all down the ages."[1] That there has been such a cry all down the ages is likely enough; but the age which tolerates it can hardly claim to be a civilized one.

[1]Mr. J. F. P. Rawlinson, in the House of Commons, November 1, 1912.

In *The Flogging Craze, a Statement of the Case against Corporal Punishment,*[1] a book published for the Humanitarian League in 1916, with a preface by my friend Sir George Greenwood, I availed myself of the large amount of material amassed by the League during its long campaign against flogging, in the hope that such a work — the first of its kind, if pamphlets be excepted — might prove useful to many social reformers, who, though instinctively opposed to the use of the lash, are often silenced by confident assertions of its efficacy, and are unaware that in this, as in similar discussions, humanity and reason go hand in hand.

Let me now turn to another and still more gruesome form of torture. It is fitting, perhaps, that the twin tyrannies of Flogging and Vivisection should be linked together as Lawson Tait saw them, for they are indeed kindred expressions of one barbarous spirit. I use, for the sake of brevity and convenience, the customary term "vivisection," though there is force in the objection raised against it by certain humanitarian writers, that the Latin word somewhat conceals the vileness of the practice, and though the phrase suggested by Mr. Howard Williams, "experimental torture," is more strictly appropriate to the nameless thing for which a name has to be found. Here, at any rate, in the twentieth century of our barbarism, is torture in its most naked form — the rack, not indeed "without any of its intellectual reasons," as was said of the lash, but torture as surely as the boot and the thumbscrew were torture. As for the intellectual reasons alleged in excuse of the practice, it was pointed out in *Animals' Rights* that before holding vivisection justified on the strength of its utility, a wise man will take into consideration the other, the *moral* side of the question, "the hideous injustice of torturing a sentient animal, and the wrong thereby done to the humane sense of the community." This contention was quoted and corroborated in an unexpected quarter, viz. in a book published in 1901 by a Russian doctor, V. Veresaeff,[2] who, though himself justifying vivisection, did not conceal his misgivings as to the ethical aspect of the practice. "The question," he said, in reference to the passage in *Animals' Rights*, "is plainly put, and there can be no room for any equivocation. I repeat that we ought not to ridicule the pretensions of the anti-vivisectionists — the

[1]London: George Allen & Unwin, Ltd.
[2]*The Confessions of a Physician*, translated by Simeon Linden, pp. 158, 159.

83

sufferings of animals are truly horrible; and sympathy with them is not sentimentality." In view of that admission, I will waste no words in discussing the pretence that anaesthetics have relieved the vivisected animals of their "truly horrible" sufferings. It is not so, even in this country, where the legal restrictions are a farce; and if it were so here, the rest of the world would be open to experimentation unlicensed and unlimited.

The special application of the word "vivisection" to physiological experiments has led to a belief, in many minds, that the vivisecting scientist is the sole torturer of animals. This is unjust both to the laboratory and to its victims. The crusade against vivisection would be much strengthened if those who take part in it would remember that the cruelties of science are only part of the great sum of cruelty that in various forms disgraces the dealings of mankind with the lower animals. Granted that the worst barbarities of the vivisector exceed those of the sportsman or the slaughterman, both in duration and intensity, it is still a fact, as scientists have often pointed out, that there are other tortures than those of the laboratory, and that to some of these the name "vivisection" might as accurately be applied. For example, clumsy castration of domestic animals, as the law is beginning to recognize, is nothing less than "farmyard vivisection"; the "docking" of horses' tails is vivisection in a very revolting form; in the seal-fishery the wretched victims of "fashion" have often been skinned alive; nor can it be pretended that the torture of the egrets, flung aside to die when their nuptial plumes have been torn off, demands a milder name than vivisection; yet some zoophilists, who look upon a vivisecting physiologist as a fiend, do not hesitate to wear an aigrette or a sealskin cloak, or to be the owners of docked horses or cropped dogs. It is impossible to draw a strict line of division between those barbarities which amount to torture, and those which fall short of it, and it is convenient that the cruelties of sport and fashion should be dealt with under a separate head; nevertheless there is one other practice on which a few words must be spoken before this chapter is closed.

Under the antiquated methods of transport and butchery still permitted in England, it is impossible to doubt that something not far removed from torture is often practised in the cattle trade; for which reason, while aware that in vegetarianism lies the only full solution of the diet-question, humanitarians have long pressed for an amelioration of the worst features of cattle-ship and shambles, and, as a minimum, for the establishment of public abattoirs in place of private slaughterhouses. Even in this respect, owing to the supineness of the County Council, London has been left at the mercy of "the trade," though in some other districts there has been a gratifying improvement. The Humanitarian League, enjoying the advantage of being advised by such experts as Sir Benjamin Richardson, Mr. H. F. Lester (whose *Behind the Scenes in Slaughterhouses* we published in 1892), Mr. Charles W. Forward, Mr. C. Cash, and Mr. R. S. Ayling, lost no opportunity of making known the need of this long postponed reform; but the subject being so repulsive it was always difficult to enlist the sympathies of the public, that is, of the very persons whose conscience ought to have been touched; or, if any interest *was* awakened, it might be among those who were traditionally or professionally opposed to the changes desired.

This danger was once curiously illustrated at a meeting held by the League in the rooms of the Royal Society for the Prevention of Cruelty to Animals, when Mr. John Colam, the Secretary of that Society, took the chair, and Mr. C. W. Forward gave an address on the Jewish method of slaughtering. A mere handful of our friends attended, but the hall was packed from end to end with Jewish visitors, who had seen the announcement of the meeting in the papers, and rallied to the defence of their ritual. We had intended to move a resolution, strongly condemning the Jewish system, but we decided, after a hurried consultation with Mr. Colam, that an academic discussion would better suit the circumstances; and fortunately it did not occur to our Hebrew friends to propose and pass a resolution of the contrary kind: they talked long and volubly, and we were glad they did nothing worse. The meeting, however, was not without result, for it led, a couple of months later, to the reception by the Jewish Board of Shecheta of a deputation from the Humanitarian League, at which the Chief Rabbi, Dr. Adler, was present, and gave us a very courteous reply. The Jewish system of "casting," he said, which had especially been criticized as barbarous, was a good deal misunderstood owing to the word by which it was described: in reality the animals were not "cast," but "let down gently with ropes." Mr. Forward, however, who had often witnessed the process, remained unconvinced on this point: it seemed to him that it was the public that was being let down gently with words.

The League had the satisfaction of seeing the Jewish system strongly condemned in the official report (1904) of the Committee appointed to consider the Humane Slaughtering of Animals; but nothing has yet been done to carry the recommendations of that Committee into effect, the supposed sanctity of a "religious" usage having been allowed, as usual, to outweigh the clearest dictates of humaneness.

There are not a few other current and strongly-rooted practices to which the title of this chapter might justly be applied; but enough has now been said to show that the merry month of May, in the year of grace 1640, did not witness, as has been supposed, quite the last instance of the infliction of Torture in this favoured land of the free.

*Seventy Years Among Savages*

# SALT ON HUNTING AND ON MURDEROUS MILLINERY

## The Deer Departed

### An Elegy

By a follower of the late Royal Buckhounds, on the King's Deer shot at Swinley Paddocks, April 12th, 1901, when the Hunt had been abolished.

Alas, poor Deer! what cruel hand
    Thy life has thus cut short?
Plague on the faddist crew that bann'd
    Our pleasant harmless sport?

No more uncarted at the Meet,
    The proudest of the proud,
Thou'lt frolic through suburban street,
    Pursued by Cockney crowd;

No more, where grassy banks invite,
    By some sweet railway-side,
The friendly playful hounds will bite
    Raw pieces from thy hide;

Nor to thy cart, so snug and warm,
    The huntsmen will convey
Thy precious blood-besprinkled form,
    "Saved for another day."

But I, who loved thee—by thy grave
    I linger broken-hearted,
And sing this sad funeral stave
    To mourn my Deer departed.

Didst wonder, since my love was such,
    I hunted thee so sore?
I could not love thee, Deer, so much,
    Loved I not Hunting more.

*Consolations of a Faddist*

What we must unhesitatingly condemn is the blind and reckless barbarism which has ransacked, and is ransacking, whole provinces and continents, without a glimmer of suspicion that the birds and quadrupeds which it is rapidly exterminating have any other part or purpose in nature than to be sacrificed to human vanity, that idle gentlemen and ladies may bedeck themselves, like certain characters in the fable, in borrowed skins and feathers. What care *they* for all the beauty and tenderness and intelligence of the varied forms of animal life? And what is it to them whether these be helped forward by man in the universal progress and evolution of all living things, or whether whole species be transformed and degraded by the way — boiled down, like the beaver, into a hat, or, like the seal, into a lady's jacket?

From *Animals' Rights*

### Hunnish Sports and Fashions

Half ignorant, they turn'd an easy wheel,
That set sharp racks at work, to pinch and peel.
KEATS

From the subject of torture we pass naturally to that of sport; indeed, it is difficult to separate them, for they are psychologically and actually akin. There is undoubtedly an element of sport in the gloating over savage punishments, and some of the sufferings which sportsmen inflict, such as the hunting to death of a timid deer or hare, cannot fairly be distinguished from torture. But when I speak of "sport" in this connection, I mean of course *blood-sport*; not the manly games of playing-field or river, but the quest for personal recreation at the expense of pain to others. The term "blood-sports" was first used, as far as I am aware, by Mr. John Macdonald, who, under the name of "Meliorist," was the author of some suggestive articles that appeared in the *Echo*; anyhow, the Humanitarian League borrowed the word from him, and finding that it "went home," made a point of using it on every possible occasion. It is the right and proper expression for the practices which it connotes.

The League published in 1914 a volume of essays on *Killing for Sport*, with Preface by Mr. Bernard Shaw, in which the various aspects of blood-sports were for the first time fully set forth and examined from the standpoint of ethics and economics: the book, in fact, formed a summary of the League's arraignment of certain bloody and barbarous pastimes, just as *The Flogging Craze* was a record of its protests against the continued use of the lash. I will here mention only a few of the more salient features of a long campaign.

For ten years, from 1891 to 1901, the League made the Royal Buckhounds serve as a "peg" — and a very useful peg it was — on which to hang an exposure of the cruelty of stag-hunting.[1] The doings of the Buckhounds were watched from season to season; detailed accounts of the "runs" were published, in contradiction of the shuffling reports sent to the papers by patrons of the Hunt, and a number of horrible cases of mutilation were dragged into light. Questions were put in Parliament; leaflets, articles, and press letters printed in hundreds, and many lectures given at various clubs and institutions.

In this work we had the sympathy of many distinguished public men and the support of a section of the press (notably of the *Star*, which was then edited by Mr. Ernest Parke); but every possible difficulty was put in our way by officials, whether of the Court, the Government, or the Hunt, who in this case, as in all, desired nothing more than to save themselves trouble by letting things go on as before. Red tape cared little whether carted stags continued to be disembowelled on iron palings and worried by hounds. For example, when, in 1898, we wished to lay before Queen Victoria the case *against* the Royal Hunt, in answer to Lord Ribblesdale's book, *The Queen's Hounds*, her private secretary, Sir A. Bigge, refused to bring the League's publications to her notice; the Home Secretary also declined to do so, and so did the Prime Minister, each and all of them cordially advising us to apply elsewhere. Thus thwarted, we hit on the expedient of *petitioning* the Queen to allow the counter-case to be sent to her, and in this way the Home Office was finally forced to do what it had declared to be "contrary to practice." The Queen, as we had known since 1891, from a private letter addressed to Mr. Stratton by Sir Henry Ponsonby, had been "strongly opposed to stag-hunting for many years past"; and when this fact was published after her death it settled the fate of the Buckhounds.

[1] A Member of Parliament who had charge of a Sports Bill once begged us not to get the Buckhounds abolished, because, as he said, they were the great incentive to vote for the Bill.

Looking back twenty years and more, it is comical to find the followers of the Royal Hunt trying to exploit the visit of the German Emperor, in 1899, in order to bolster up the failing reputation of their sport. They were very anxious that a "meet" of the Buckhounds should be one of the entertainments provided for the Kaiser, and on November 24th, in expectation of his being present, an unusually large company assembled; but the Humanitarian League had been beforehand in the matter, a letter of protest which it had addressed to the Prince of Wales had the desired effect, and the Kaiser had an engagement elsewhere. Had he been present, he would, as it happened, have seen a deer staked and done to death in the manner which was far from uncommon, and he would have learnt (if he had any doubt on the subject) that "Huns" are not entirely confined to Germany.

This rascally "sport," though no longer a State institution, is still carried on by private packs in several parts of the country, and nothing but fresh legislation can prevent its continuance. A "Spurious Sports Bill" drafted by the Humanitarian League, with the purpose of prohibiting the hunting of carted stags, the coursing of bagged rabbits, and the shooting of birds released from traps, has been introduced at various times in the House of Commons by Mr. A. C. Morton, Mr. H. F. Luttrell, Sir William Byles, Sir George Greenwood, and other Members, and in the House of Lords by the Bishop of Hereford (Dr. Percival); but its opponents have always succeeded in preventing its becoming law. On one occasion (1893) it was "talked out" by Sir Frederick Banbury, who is renowned in the House as an anti-vivisectionist and friend of animals. It is not only human beings who have to pray, at times, to be delivered from their friends.

The Eton Beagles were another of the League's most cherished "pegs," and displayed as useful an illustration of the hare-hunt as the Royal Buckhounds of the deer-worry. Had humanitarians talked of the cruelty of hare-hunting in general, little attention would have been paid to them; but with concrete instances drawn from the leading public school, and quoted in the words of the boys themselves as printed in the *Eton College Chronicle* — a disgusting record of "blooded" hounds and of the hare "broken up," or crawling "dead-beat," "absolutely stiff," "so done that she could not stand" — a great impression was made, and the memorials presented to the headmaster or the Governing Body, asking for the substitution of a drag-hunt (a form of sport which was formerly popular at Eton and led to very good runs), received a large number of very influential signatures, including that of the Visitor of Eton, the late Bishop of Lincoln, Dr. E. L. Hicks. But public opinion counts for very little at the school where ignorance is bliss; a far more important consideration for Governing Bodies and headmasters is the opinion of Old Etonians; indeed, it is doubtful whether a headmaster of Eton could even retain his position if he were to decree the discontinuance of what Dr. Warre described, with all due solemnity, as "an old Eton institution." So obvious was this that we were inspired to borrow the title of Gray's famous poem in an enlarged form, and to indite an "Ode on the Exceedingly Distant Prospect of Humane Reform at Eton College."

Dr. E. C. Selwyn, headmaster of Uppingham, wrote to me if he were made headmaster of Eton, he would abolish the Beagles "at the earliest opportunity." Unfortunately he was not the successful candidate for the post when Dr. Warre gave it up, or we might have seen some rare sport at Eton, and a hue and cry more exciting than any hare-hunt. Dislike of blood-sport as a school recreation is by no means confined to humanitarians, as may be seen from the following sentence which I quote from an interesting unpublished letter on the ethics of sport, addressed to Mr. Stratton in 1905 by Mr. F. C. Selous, the great lion-hunter: "After reading your pamphlet, I certainly think it would be better to substitute drag-hunting for the pursuit and killing of a hare. To see one of these animals worried and torn by a pack of dogs is not an edifying sight for a young boy."

All hunting, whether of the hare, fox, stag, or otter, has many horrible features: perhaps the very nastiest is the custom of "blooding," i.e. baptizing with the blood of the mangled victim any children or young folk who partake in the sport for the first time. The practice has been described, but too modestly, it would seem, as "a hunting tradition which goes back to the Middle Ages"; one would suppose it went back to still more primitive times. Yet to this day this savage ritual is patronized by our nobility and by royalty. "Prince Henry was blooded," was the conclusion of a newspaper report of a "kill" with a pack of foxhounds, January 9, 1920. There is a double significance, it seems, in the expression "a prince of the blood."

"You can't eliminate cruelty from sport," says a distinguished sportsman, the Earl of Warwick, in his *Memories of Sixty Years*. In no form of blood-sport do we more clearly see what a veritable mania this amateur butchery may become than in one of Lord Warwick's hobbies, "big game hunting," the difficult and costly pursuit of wild animals in distant lands, for no better reason than the craze for killing. Tiger-shooting is doubtless an exciting pastime, and there are savage beasts that at times have to be destroyed; but what of that other tiger that lurks in the heart of each of us? And how is *he* going to be eliminated, so long as a savage lust for killing is a recognized form of amusement? For in spite of all the barriers and divisions that prejudice and superstition have heaped up between the human and the non-human, we may take it as certain that, in the long run, as we treat our fellow-beings, "the animals," so shall we treat our fellow-men.

Every one knows how the possessors of such "trophies" as the heads and horns of "big game" love to decorate their halls with these mementoes of the chase. I was once a visitor at a house which was not only adorned in this way, but contained also a human head that had been sent home by a member of a certain African expedition and "preserved" by the skill of the taxidermist. When I was invited by the owner of the head — the *second* owner — to see that particular trophy, it was with some misgivings that I acquiesced; but when, after passing up a staircase between walls plastered with portions of the carcases of elephant, rhinoceros, antelope, etc., I came to a landing where, under a glass case, was the head of a pleasant-looking young negro, I felt no special repugnance at the sight. It was simply a part — and, as it seemed, not a peculiarly dreadful or loathsome part — of the surrounding dead-house; and I understood how mankind itself may be nothing more than "big game" to our soldier-sportsmen abroad. The absolute distinction between human and non-human is a fiction which will not bear the test either of searching thought in the study or of rough experience in the wilds.

Iniquitous as the Game Laws are, I have often thought it strange that Kingsley, even when regarding them, quite justly, from the poacher's standpoint, should have hurled at the game-preserver that eloquent denunciation:

> There's blood on the game you sell, squire,
> And there's blood on the game you eat,

without in the least realizing the full truth of the statement. For there, literally, is blood on the "game" which the squire (or the poacher) disposes of, viz. the blood of the "game" itself; and that Kingsley should have forgotten this, is a singular proof of the way in which the lower animals are regarded as mere goods and chattels, and not as creatures of flesh and blood at all — except to cook and eat. The very use of the word "game," in this sense, is most significant.

As mention has been made of the fall of the Royal Buckhounds, a few words must be said of the man who chiefly brought it about. The Rev. J. Stratton was Master of Lucas's Hospital, Wokingham, a charitable institution founded in 1663, where a number of aged labourers live as pensioners; and as Wokingham lay in the centre of the hunting district, he was well placed for observing what went on, and for obtaining exact information: he had, moreover, a first-hand knowledge of "sport," and his detestation of it was based on his own earlier experiences, as well as on a keen sense of fair play. Of all the active workers with whom I have been privileged to be associated, Mr. Stratton was the finest; I have known nothing more courageous than the way in which, almost single-handed at first, and with the whole hunting fraternity against him, he gradually "pulled down" (to use a pleasant sporting term) the cruel and stupid institution which was carried on in the Sovereign's name and at the expense of the public.

In character, as in appearance, Mr. Stratton was a Roman; his stern and unswerving rectitude made him respected even by his most active opponents. His outspokenness, where matters of real import were at stake, was quite undaunted, and to an extent which sometimes caused consternation among the weaker brethren. I was once asked by a sympathetic bishop whether it would be possible "to keep Mr. Stratton quiet." More than one dignitary of the Church must have mused on that problem; for if Mr. Stratton had a weakness, it was for a bishop. I do not mean that he viewed bishops with undue reverence, somewhat the reverse, for he loved to take a bishop to task; and some of his letters to bishops, in reference to their sanction of vivisection or blood-sports, were of a nature to cause a mild surprise in episcopal circles. But if bishops did not always appreciate Mr. Stratton, other persons did. So well did the birds in his garden at Woking-ham understand him, that they would let him talk to them and stroke them as they sat on their nests. Could there be a more convincing proof of a man's goodness?

Another active champion of the reform of blood-sports was Colonel W. L. B. Coulson, a well-known Northumberland country gentleman and J.P., who was one of the first men of influence to join the Humanitarian League. He possessed a fine military presence, and a voice which, even at its whisper, had a volume and resonance which could not fail to make it heard to the uttermost corner of a room; his appearance, in brief, had so little of the pale cast of thought that on the occasion when he first met us we were the victims of an odd misapprehension. It had been arranged that he would preside at a public meeting in London, the first we held, on the subject of deer-hunting; and when the members of our Committee arrived, some time before the discussion began, we were troubled to find thus early upon the scene a very large and powerfully built man, whom, as he did not introduce himself, we imagined to be a master of staghounds, or at least an opponent of formidable calibre, come to intimidate us at the start. We were relieved when we discovered him to be our missing chairman.

Colonel Coulson was very popular with his audiences, for there was a frankness about him which went straight to the heart, and his speeches, though not cultured, were full of raciness and humanity. Himself brought up as a sportsman, he felt keenly about the sufferings of animals, and after his retirement from the army devoted much time to lecturing-tours, in which he visited many parts of the country and especially addressed himself to schools. Eton would not receive him, doubtless fearing some reference to her hare-hunt; but at several of the other big public schools he was asked to speak more than once. Brave, simple, and courteous, he was loved by all who knew him, and by none more than by his colleagues in the humanitarian cause.

Nothing was more remarkable in the history of the Humanitarian League than the diversity of character in the persons whom its principles attracted. Lady Florence Dixie, who joined the League at its start in 1891, had a strange and adventurous career, and has been described, not inaptly, as ''a sort of 'Admirable Crichton' among women, a poet, a novelist, an explorer, a war correspondent, a splendid horse-woman, a convincing platform-speaker, a swimmer of great endurance, and as keen a humanitarian as ever lived." It was as humanitarian that I knew her; and she was certainly one of the most faithful supporters of the League, ever ready to help with pen or purse, and prompt, sincere, and unwavering in her friendship. Her poems, of which she sent me more than one volume, had little worth; but her essay on "The Horrors of Sport" was one of the most vivid and moving appeals that have been written on the subject; none of the League's pamphlets had so wide a circulation, for it has been read and quoted in every part of the English-speaking world. She here wrote with full knowledge of the facts, and with a sympathetic insight, which, together with a swift and picturesque style, made her, at her best, a powerful and fascinating writer. Of her personal eccentricities many reports were rife; and I remembered that when I lived at Eton she used to be seen in the garden of her villa, on the Windsor bank of the Thames, walking, like a modern Circe, with a number of wild beasts in her train. On one occasion a jaguar made his escape from her control, and there was a mild panic in Windsor and Eton till he was recaptured: it might have indeed been serious if the bold youths who hunted the terror-stricken hare had started a quarry that showed fight.

Another unfailing friend of the League's Sports Committee was the Hon. FitzRoy Stewart. When I first knew him he was Secretary of the Central Conservative Office, and we were rather surprised at finding an ally in that direction; in fact, we had some suspicions, entirely unjust, as the result proved, that Mr. Stewart might be desirous of learning our plan of campaign against the Royal Buckhounds in the interest of his sporting friends. The first time I visited him at the Conservative headquarters I was introduced to Sir Howard Vincent, M.P., who, though a patron of the Royal Society for the Prevention of Cruelty to Animals, had not scrupled to throw in his lot with those who were fighting for the continuance of rabbit-coursing, pigeon-shooting and stag-hunting. He seemed to be a good-natured, vacuous-minded person, and one of his remarks, I remember, was that England is "a paradise for animals." This was hardly the opinion of FitzRoy Stewart, who was indefatigable with his schemes for the prohibition of the more cruel forms of sport. He had great hopes of young Mr. Winston Churchill, then beginning to be known as a rising star of the Tory party, and at his earnest request a letter was sent to Mr. Churchill from the office of the League, reminding him of Lord Randolph Churchill's strong denunciation of stag-hunting, and asking his aid against the Buckhounds. Mr. Churchill, however, unmoved by this appeal to his filial piety, sagely opined that the crusade against the Royal Hunt was too democratic.

Mr. FitzRoy Stewart worked closely with the Humanitarian League till his death in 1914; and many were his press letters which he and I jointly composed at the office in Chancery Lane. He liked to come there armed with some sheets of his Carlton Club notepaper, on which the letters, when worded to his satisfaction, were duly copied and signed — "Old Harrovian," or "A Member of the Carlton Club," was his favourite signature — and then he sent them off to some influential editors of his acquaintance, whose disgust would have been unmeasured had they known what company their esteemed contributor had been keeping. Mr. Stewart, I must in fairness add, though a strong opponent of blood-sport, was a firm believer in the beneficence of flogging; but he was willing to sink this one point of difference in his general approval of the League's work. So good-natured was he, that when the subject of corporal punishment was going to crop up at a Committee meeting, he used to ask me to put it first on the agenda, so that he might wait outside until that burning question was disposed of: then he would join us — coming in to dessert, as we expressed it — and take his share in the discussion. Oh, if all colleagues were as reasonable! As *The Times* truly said of him, "his sweetness of temper and social tact made him the most companionable of human beings."

Mr. John Colam, for many years Secretary of the Royal Society for the Prevention of Cruelty to Animals, was a well-known figure in the zoophilist movement at the time of which I am speaking, and had a great reputation for astuteness. Wily he certainly was, with the vast experience he had acquired in evading the double pressure of those who cried "forward" and of those who cried "back"; and he was a veritable Proteus in the skill with which he gave the slip to any one who tried to commit him to any course but the safest. He used privately to allege the backwardness of his Committee as a cause for this seeming timidity; thus he told me in 1901, when the fate of the Royal Buckhounds was hanging in the balance, that the R.S.P.C.A. was unable to take any public action, not from any remissness on his part, but because certain members of the Committee were afraid of alienating subscribers, including King Edward himself. Personally I liked Mr. Colam; he was humane so far as his interests permitted, and when one had realized, once for all, the uselessness of attempting to bind him to any fixed purpose, it was instructive to have an occasional talk with him at Jermyn Street, and to observe the great adroitness with which he conducted the affairs of the Society; and he, on his part, when he saw that one had no longer any ethical designs on him, but approached him rather as a fellow-student, albeit a mere amateur, in the art of dealing with unreasonable people, would become chatty and confidential and tell amusing stories of a Secretary's adventures. He would have made a successful Prime Minister, for his "wizardry" was of the highest order; as a humanitarian he left something to be desired.

With the Sporting League, which professed to discountenance "malpractices" in sport, yet opposed the Bill which would have prohibited rabbit-coursing and kindred pastimes, we were of course involved in controversy. We sought to bring this to a point by proposing a public discussion of the question: "What are malpractices in Sport?" But this challenge was declined, the *Sportsman* expressing the opinion that "such piffling folly is best treated with contempt," and the *Evening News* that "cackling is the strong point of the faddists." We were more successful in bringing to book some champions of aristocratic blood-sports, among them Sir Herbert Maxwell and Sir Edward Grey, who on one or two occasions appeared on neutral platforms, and seized the opportunity to eulogize their own favourite recreations, but showed little relish for the discussion which they themselves had provoked. Mr. F. G. Aflalo was another of our many antagonists in the magazines and the press; and I have a pleasant recollection of friendly encounters with him in the *Fortnightly Review* and elsewhere. Many other apologists of blood-sports there were, of a more sentimental and unreasoning kind, and with these, too, we much enjoyed the argument, which was quite as good sport to us as their hunting or coursing was to them.

Before passing from Sports to Fashions, I will speak briefly of those popular places of recreation, known euphemistically as "Zoological Gardens," which in a civilized age would surely be execrated as among the saddest and dullest spots on the earth, being, in fact, nothing cheerier than big convict-stations, to which the ill-fated life-prisoners — "stuff," as the keepers call them — are conveyed from many distant lands. How any rational person can find pleasure in seeing, for example, "the lions fed" (the modern version of *Christianos ad leones*) is a mystery that baffles thought. I have not been to the London "Zoo" for a good many years; but when I knew it, the incongruities of the place were so ludicrous as almost to obscure one's sense of its barbarity: the Tiger's den, for instance, was labelled: "Beware of pickpockets," and the Eagle's cage bore the inscription: "To the Refreshment Rooms"; and there, sure enough, within sight of the captive Bird of Jove moping disconsolate on his perch, was a waiter, serving out coffees or lemon-squashes, regardless of the great Raptor by whom his predecessor, Ganymede, had been carried off to be the god's cup-bearer. Could bathos have gone further?

A friend of mind who, as an Eton boy, used to go to the "Zoo" in the holidays and amuse himself by teasing the captives, was converted to humanitarian principles in a rather curious way. An elk, or some large animal of the ruminant order, whose wrath he had deservedly incurred, *coughed* on him with such vehemence that he retired from the elk-house covered with a sort of moist bran, and with his top-hat irrevocably damaged. Though at the time this touched his hat rather than his heart, he afterwards came to regard the incident as what is called a "means of grace." It caused *him*, too, to "ruminate," and so brought home to him the fact that an elk is "a person."

A pamphlet of mine, issued by the Humanitarian League in 1895, entitled "A Zoophilist at the Zoo," was the beginning of an agitation which gradually led to a considerable improvement in the housing of the animals, in which discussion the most noteworthy feature was a series of articles contributed to the *Saturday Review* by Mr. Edmund Selous, and afterwards reprinted by the League. Another subject, debated with much liveliness, was the practice of feeding pythons and other large serpents on living prey — ducks, fowls, rabbits, and even goats being given to the reptiles, to be devoured in a manner which was sickening to witness and almost too loathsome to describe.[1] These exhibitions were open till 1881; then for publicity extreme secrecy was substituted, and all inquiries were met by the stereotyped

[1] See Dickens's description, Forster's *Life of Dickens*, iii, 146.

statement that the use of live prey was confined to cases "where such food was a necessity."

Who feeds slim serpents must himself be slim.

The League found the reptile-feeders at Regent's Park exceedingly slippery to deal with, and it needed long time, and much patience, to bring them to book. In this task, however, I was encouraged by the recollection of a scene which I once witnessed in a crowded railway-carriage, when a large eel had made its escape from a basket which one of my fellow-travellers was holding, and created a mild panic among the company by its convolutions under the seat. An old lady sharply upbraided the owner of the eel, and I was struck by the reasonableness of his reply in rather difficult circumstances, when the eel had repeatedly slipped from his grasp. "Wait a little, mum," he said, "until he gets a bit dusty"; and the result proved the man to be right. In like manner we waited till the excuses given by the Zoological Society had become very dusty indeed.

Some of the reasons offered for the old system of snake-feeding were themselves truly reptilian. "We follow God's ordinances, and they must be right," was the reverent remark of a keeper; and humanitarians were told that "to declare the use of live food to be cruel is to bring that charge against the Designer of Nature Himself." So deep and fervent was the piety of the Reptile House! Nevertheless, we continued to urge our point, and the subject was hotly debated at more than one of the Zoological Society's annual meetings, where, as a result of the protests raised by Captain Alfred Carpenter, R.N., Mr. Stephen Coleridge, Mr. Rowland Hunt, and other F.Z.S.'s, it was made evident that the majority of the Fellows, who regarded the Society as a sort of private club, were indignant at public opinion being brought to bear upon their concerns. It was a situation not devoid of humour. I happen to know that in the course of an excited meeting held in November, 1907, when the Duke of Bedford, as President of the Zoological Society, was in the chair, the following telegram was despatched to his Grace:

Beg you to stand firm for live food and maintain the ordinances of the Creator.

From *Anna Conda.*

This artless prayer of an unknown lady was fully in accord with the spirit of the meeting. Nevertheless, things moved, even in Regent's Park; and, when we had shown that the snakes in the New York Zoological Park were successfully fed on freshly-killed animals, we had the satisfaction of seeing the same less barbarous method adopted at the London "Zoo."

I once had the advantage of hearing some of the inner history of a large menagerie from the wife of one of the keepers, a charwoman in the house where I was staying, who was of a somewhat loquacious and communicative disposition, the staple of her talk being the adventures of her husband, Johnnie. "Johnnie came home dead-tired last night, sir," she said on one occasion. "Why was that, Mrs. Smith?" I asked. "Why, sir, he had had to beat the elephant; and after that he was too stiff and tired to take his supper." My natural inquiry whether the elephant had been able to take *his* supper was set aside as frivolous.

Knowing something of the profound piety of the keepers at the (London) "Zoo" in relation to snake-feeding, I was pained to learn from this good woman that her husband, who, unfortunately, was not employed in a reptile-department, had "lost his faith," and for a reason which I think has not before been recorded among the many modern causes of unbelief. "You see, sir, Johnny can never again hold with the Church, after the way he's seen clergymen going on with girls in the elephant house."

When speaking of cruel pastimes, I referred to the value of the term "blood-sports" in the many controversies which we waged. Just as the fortunes of a book may be affected by its title, so in ethical and political discussions there is often what may be called a winning word; and where none such is found ready to hand, it is advisable to invent one. Thus the League made good play with "flagellomania," as used by Mr. Bernard Shaw in one of his lectures; and "brutalitarian" (an invention of our own, I think) did us yeoman service, as will be seen in a later chapter. "Murderous Millinery," another term which has gained a wide circulation, was first used as a chapter-heading in my *Animals' Rights*; and though it rather shocked some zoophilists of the older school, who presumably thought that only a human being can be "murdered," it served a useful purpose, perhaps, in drawing attention to the revolting cruelty that underlies the plumage trade. In its condemnation of these barbarities, as in other matters, the Humanitarian League was a pioneer; its pamphlet on "The Extermination of Birds," written by Miss Edith Carrington, and published nearly thirty years ago, played a marked part in the creation of a better public opinion; and a Bill drafted by the League in 1901, to prohibit the use of the plumage of certain rare and beautiful birds, attracted very wide public attention, and was the basis of subsequent attempts at legislation. But here it must be added that the man who has done more than all the Societies together to insure the passage of a Plumage Bill is Mr. James Buckland. Nothing in the humanitarian movement has been finer than the way in which Mr. Buckland forced this question to the front and made it peculiarly his own.

Every whit as savage as the feather-trade is the fur-trade, responsible as it is for some most horrible methods of torture — the steel-trap, which inflicts shocking injuries on its victim; the spring-pole, which jerks both trap and captive high in air, there to hang till the trapper next comes on his rounds; the terrible "dead-fall" used for bears and other large animals; the poisoning of wolves with strychnine; and the abominations in the butchery of seals. Even the fashionable people who wear furs (in a climate where there is not the least need of such clothing) would hardly be able to continue the habit if they knew how their "comforts" were provided; as it is, the Feather-Headed Woman is not a commoner sight in our streets than the Ass in the skin of the (Sea) Lion. It would seem that fur-wearers are almost unconscious that their sables and sealskins are the relics of previous possessors, and, like the heroines of modern drama, have very decidedly had "a past"; or, if they do not wholly forget this fact, they think it quite natural that *they* should now have their turn with the skin, as the animal had before. Thus Pope, in a well-known couplet:

> Know, Nature's children all divide her care;
> The fur that warms a monarch warmed a bear.

One would have thought that the bear who grew the skin had somewhat more right to it than the monarch! Politicians may talk of "one man, one vote"; but really, if there is ever to be a civilized state, a programme of "one man, one skin" seems fairer and more democratic.

*Seventy Years Among Savages*

# II
# SALT AS NATURALIST
# AND CONSERVATIONIST

## NATURALIST

### To C.L.S.[1]

I send thee, love, this upland flower I found,
While wandering lonely with o'erclouded heart,
Hid in a grey recess of rocky ground
Among the misty mountains far apart;
And there I heard the wild wind's luring sound,
Which whoso trusts, is healed of earthborn care,
And watched the lofty ridges loom around,
Yet yearned in vain their secret faith to share.
When lo! the sudden sunlight, sparkling keen,
Poured full upon the vales the glorious day,
And bared the abiding mountain-tops serene,
And swept the shifting vapour-wreaths away:—
Then with the hills' true heart my heart beat true,
Heavens opened, cloud-thoughts vanished, and I knew.

*On Cambrian and Cumbrian Hills*

[1]Salt's wife, Catherine Leigh Salt.

## *The Call of the Wildflower*

*Tantus amor florum.*—VIRGIL

The ''call of the wild,'' where the love of flowers is concerned, has an attraction which is not the less powerful because it is difficult to explain. The charm of the garden may be strong, but it is not so strong as that which draws us to seek for wildflowers in their native haunts, whether of shore or water-meadow, field or wood, moorland or mountain. A garden is but a ''zoo'' (with the cruelty omitted); and just as the true natural history is that which sends us to study animals in the wilds, not to coop them in cages, so the true botany must bring man to the flower, not the flower to man.

That the lovers of wildflowers — those, at least, who can give active expression to their love — are not a numerous folk, is perhaps not surprising; for even a moderate knowledge of the subject demands such favourable conditions as free access to nature, with opportunities for observation beyond what most persons command; but what they lack in numbers they make up in zeal, and to none is the approach of spring more welcome than to those who are then on the watch for the reappearance of floral friends.

For it is as friends, not garden captives or herbarium specimens, that the flower-lover desires to be acquainted with flowers. It is not their uses that attract him; *that* is the business of the herbalist. Nor is it their structure and analysis; the botanist will see to that. What he craves is a knowledge of the loveliness, the actual life and character of plants in their relation to man — what may be called the spiritual aspect of flowers — and this is seen and felt much more closely when they are sought in their free wild state than when they are cultivated on rockery or in parterre.

The reality of this love of wildflowers is evident, but its cause and meaning are less easy to discern. Is it only part of a modern ''return to nature,'' or a sign of some latent sympathy between plant and man? We do not know; but we know that our interest in flowers is no longer utilitarian, as in the herbalism of a bygone time, or decorative and aesthetic, as in the immemorial use of the garland on festive occasions, and in the association of the wine-cup with the rose. The ''great affection'' that Chaucer felt for the daisy marked a new era; and later poets have carried the sentiment still further, till it reached a climax in the faith that Wordsworth avowed:

> One impulse from a vernal wood
> May teach you more of man,
> Of moral evil and of good,
> Than all the sages can.

Here is a new herbalism — of the heart. We smile nowadays at the credulity of the old physicians, who rated so highly the virtues of certain plants as to assert, for example, that comfrey — the "great consound," as they called it — had actual power to unite and solidify a broken bone. But how if there be flowers that can in very truth make whole a broken spirit? Even in the Middle Ages it was recognized that mental benefit was to be gained from this source, as when betony was extolled for its value in driving away despair, and when *fuga daemonum* was the name given to St. John's-wort, that golden-petaled amulet which, when hung over a doorway, could put all evil spirits to flight. That, like many another flower, it can put "the blues" to flight, is a fact which no modern flower-lover will doubt.

But what may be called the anthropocentric view of wildflowers is now happily becoming obsolete. "Their beauty was given them for our delight," wrote Anne Pratt in one of the pleasantest of her books:[1] "God sent them to teach us lessons of Himself." It would somewhat spoil our joy in the beauty of wildflowers if we thought they had been "sent," like potted plants from a nursery, for any purpose whatsoever; for it is their very naturalness, their independence of man, that charms us, and our regard for them is less the prosaic satisfaction of an owner in his property, than the love of a friend, or even the worship of a devotee:

> The devotion to something afar
> From the sphere of our sorrow.

This, I think, is the true gospel of the love of flowers, though as yet it has found but little expression in the literature of the subject. "Flowers as flowers," was Thoreau's demand, when he lamented in his journal that there was no book which treated of them in that light, no real "biography" of plants. The same want

[1]*Haunts of the Wild Flowers.*

is felt by the English reader to-day: there is no writer who has done for the wildflower what Mr. W. H. Hudson has done for the bird.[1]

Indeed, the books mostly fail, not only to portray the life of the plant, but even to give an intelligible account of its habitat and appearance; for very few writers, however sound their technical knowledge, possess the gift of lucid description — a gift which depends, in its turn, upon that sympathy with other minds which enables an author to see precisely what instruction is needed. Thus it often happens that, unless personal help is available, it is a matter of great difficulty for a beginner to learn the haunts of flowers, or to distinguish them when found; for when he refers to the books he finds much talk about inessential things, and little that goes directly to the point.

One might have thought that a new and strange flower would attract the eye more readily than a known one, but it is not so; the old is detected much more easily than the new. "Out of sight, out of mind," says the proverb; and conversely that which is not yet in mind will long tarry out of sight. But when once a new flower, even a rare one, has been discovered, it is curious how often it will soon be noticed afresh in another place: this, I think, must be the experience of all who have made systematic search for flowers, and it explains why the novice will frequently see but little where the expert will see much.

Not until the various initial obstacles have been overcome can one appreciate the true "call of the wild," the full pleasures of the chase. When we have learnt not only what plants are to be looked for, but those two essential conditions, the *when* and the *where*; the rule of season and of soil; the flowers that bloom in spring, in summer, or in autumn; the flowers that grow by shore, meadow, bog, river, or mountain; on chalk, limestone, sand, or clay — then the quest becomes more effective, and each successive season will add materially to our widening circle of acquaintance.

Then, too, we may begin to discard that rather vapid class of literature, the popular flower-book, which too often deals sentimentally in vague descriptions of plants, diversified with bad illustrations, and with edifying remarks about the goodness of the Creator, and may find a new and more rational interest in

[1]Unless it be Canon John Vaughan, in those two delightful books of his, *The Wild-Flowers of Selborne* and *The Music of Wild-Flowers*.

the published *Floras* of such counties or districts as have yet received that distinction. For dry though it is in form, a *Flora*, with its classified list of plants, and its notes collected from many sources, past and present, as to their "stations" in the county, becomes an almost romantic book of adventure, when the student can supply the details from his own knowledge, and so read with illumination "between the lines." Here, let us suppose it to be said, is a locality where grows some rare and beautiful flower, one of the prizes of the chase. What hopes and aspirations such an assurance may arouse! What encouragement to future enterprise! What regrets, it may be, for some almost forgotten omission in the past, which left that very neighbourhood unsearched! It is possible that a cold, matter-of-fact entry in a local *Flora* will thus throw a sudden light on some bygone expedition, and show us that if we had but taken a slightly different direction in our walk — but it is vain to lament what is irreparable!

Of such musings upon the might-have-been I can myself speak with feeling, for I was not so fortunate in my youth as to be initiated into the knowledge of flowers: it was not till much later in life, as I wandered among the Welsh and English mountains, that the scales fell from my eyes, and looking on the beauty of the saxifrages I realized what glories I had missed. Thus I was compelled to put myself to school, so to speak, and to make a study of wildflowers with the aid of such books as were available, a process which, like a botanical Jude the Obscure, I found by no means easy. The self-educated man, we know, is apt to be perverse and opinionated; so I trust my readers will make due allowance if they notice such faults in this book. I can truly plead, as the illiterate do, that "I'm no scholar, more's the pity."

But it was my friends and acquaintances — those, at least, who had some botanical knowledge — who were the chief sufferers during this period of inquiry; and, looking back, I often marvel at the patience with which they endured the problems with which I confronted them. I remember waylaying my friend, W. J. Jupp, a very faithful flower-lover, with some mutilated and unrecognizable labiate plant which I thought might be calamint, and how tactfully he suggested that my conjecture was "near enough."

On another occasion it was Edward Carpenter, the Sage of Millthorpe, or Wild Sage, as some botanical friend once irreverently described him, who volunteered to assist me, by means of a scientific book which shows, by an unerring process, how to eliminate the wrong flowers, until at the end you are left with the right one duly named. All through the list we went; but there must have been a slip somewhere; for in the conclusion one thing alone was clear — that whatever my plant might be, it was not that which the scientific book indicated. Of all my friends and helpers, Bertram Lloyd, whose acquaintance with wildflowers is unusually large, and to whom, in all that pertains to natural history, I am as the "gray barbarian" (*vide* Tennyson) to "the Christian child," was the most constant and long-suffering: he solved many of my enigmas, and introduced me to some of his choicest flower-haunts among the Chiltern Hills.

In the course of my researches I was sometimes referred for guidance to persons who were known in their respective home-circles as "the botanists of the family," a title which I found was not quite equivalent to that of "the complete botanist." There was one "botanist of the family" who was visibly embarrassed when I asked her the name of a plant that is common on the chalk hills, but is so carelessly described in the books as to be easily confused with other kindred species. She gazed at it long, with a troubled eye, and then, as if feeling that her domestic reputation must at all hazards be upheld, replied firmly: "Hemp-nettle." Hemp-nettle it was not; it was wild basil; but years after, when I began to have similar questions put to myself, I realized how disconcerting it is to be thus suddenly interrogated. It made me understand why Cabinet Ministers so frequently insist that they must have "notice of that Question."

With one complete botanist, however, I was privileged to become acquainted, Mr. C. E. Salmon, whose special diocese, so to speak, is the county of Surrey, but whose intimate knowledge of wildflowers extends to many counties and coasts. Not a few favours did I receive from him, in certifying for me some of the more puzzling plants; and very good-naturedly he bore the disappointment when, on his asking me to send him, for his *Flora of Surrey*, a list of the rarer flowers in the neighbourhood where I was living, I included among them the small bur-parsley (*caucalis daucoides*), a vanished native, a prodigal son of the county, whose return would have been a matter for gladness. But alas, my plant was not a *caucalis* at all, but a *torilis*, a squat weed of the cornfields, which by its superficial resemblance to its rare cousin had grossly imposed upon my ignorance.

It is when he has acquired some familiarity with the ordinary British plants that a flower-lover, thus educated late in life, finds his thoughts turning to the vanished opportunities of the past. I used to speculate regretfully on what I had missed in my early wanderings in wild places; as in the Isle of Skye, where I picked up the eagle's feather, but overlooked the mountain flower; or on Ben Lawers, a summit rich in rare Alpines to which I then was stone-blind; or in a score of other localities which I can scarcely hope to revisit. But time, which heals all things, brought me a sort of compensation for these delinquencies; for with a fuller knowledge of plants I could to some extent reconstruct in imagination the sights that were formerly unseen, and with the eye of faith admire the Alpine forget-me-not on the ridges of Ben Lawers, or the yellow butterwort in the marshes of Skye. Nor was it always in my imagination only; for sometimes a friend would send me a rare flower from some distant spot; and then there was pleasure indeed in the opening of the parcel and in anticipating what it might contain — the pasque-flower perhaps, or the wild tulip, or the Adonis, or the golden samphire, or some other of the many local treasures that make glad the flower-lover's heart.

The exhibitions of wildflowers that are now held in the public libraries of not a few towns are extremely useful, and often awake a love of nature in minds where it has hitherto been but dormant. A queer remark was once made to me by a visitor at the Brighton show. "This is a good institution," he said. "It saves you from tramping for the flowers yourself." I had not regarded the exhibition in that light; on the contrary, it stimulates many persons to a pursuit which is likely to fascinate them more and more.

For no tramps can be pleasanter than those in quest of wildflowers; especially if one has a fellow-enthusiast for companion: failing that, it is wiser to go alone; for when a flower-lover tramps with someone who has no interest in the pursuit, the result is likely to be discomfiting — he must either forgo his own haltings and deviations, with the probability that he will miss something valuable, or he must feel that he is delaying his friend. In a company, I always pray that their number may be uneven, and that it may not be necessary to march stolidly in pairs, where "one to one is cursedly confined," as Dryden said of matrimony; or worst of all, where one's yoke-fellow may insist, as sometimes happens, on walking "in step," and be forever shuffling his feet as if obeying the commands of some invisible drill-sergeant. It is not with the feet that we should seek harmony, but with the heart. . . .

*The Call of the Wildflower*

Wildflowers, to my thinking, are among the friendliest of wild things. Birds, if we could make free acquaintance with them, might be still more so; but except in certain rare cases . . . they usually fly away when approached (thanks to the foolish practice of shooting at them), whereas the flowers remain for our self-introduction.

From "Friendly Wildflowers" in *Company I Have Kept*

## CONSERVATIONIST

Humanitarianism is not merely an expression of sympathy with pain: it is a protest against all tyranny and desecration, whether such wrongs be done by the infliction of suffering on sentient beings, or by the Vandalism which can ruthlessly destroy the natural grace of the earth.

*Seventy Years Among Savages*

. . . as regards a number of rare and beautiful wildflowers, it is becoming a race between their destroyers and their saviours. . . . The rule should be, never to uproot a wildflower, and never even to pick more than are absolutely required.

*Company I Have Kept*

## *Our Vanishing Wildflowers*

"There are three classes which need sanctuary more than others — birds, wildflowers, and Prime Ministers." So said Mr. Baldwin when unveiling the Hudson memorial in Hyde Park;[1] and the remark is specially true of wildflowers, which, unlike birds, have no wings to bear them to a place of safety, and, unlike Prime Ministers, no Chequers to which they can retire from observation. A correspondence printed in *The Times* in the spring of 1925 brought the subject to the fore, and led to the issue of an appeal for protection, addressed to County Councils by the Society for the Promotion of Nature Reserves. The fact that many plants are diminishing, the rarer ones with greater rapidity, is beyond question, and the cause of the trouble is no less plain; what is not so easy to discover is an available method of saving them.

The decrease of rare or beautiful plants is in some cases unavoidable, as when it is caused by the growth of towns or by improved methods of cultivation. We are concerned only with that wanton destruction which results from thoughtlessness, cupidity, or a lack of public spirit — a failure to understand that the *flora* of a country belongs to the nation as a whole, and is of far greater importance than any private property in gardens.

Of the various practices by which the wealth of our native flora is being impaired, the simplest and most obvious is the excessive picking of blossoms by persons who do not realize, or are indifferent to the fact, that this, in the long run, must lessen the abundance of the plant. Nothing is commoner, in the spring, than to see big bunches of primroses, cowslips, bluebells, or some other flower, lying by the roadside, where they have been left by children who have picked them only to throw them aside.[2] Nor are children the sole offenders. A local reputation is often a great danger to a scarce plant; as in the case of certain orchids which, though classed among the rarities, have the doubtful advantage of being locally abundant, with the result that at the season when they are in flower they are systematically raided, and sometimes pulled so clumsily that the life of the plant is endangered. The

[1]*The Times*, May 20, 1925.
[2]"A fortnight ago it was no uncommon thing to see a string of motor-cars, including a motor-coach or two, drawn up alongside a patch of bluebells, and all the occupants as busy as could be, picking, uprooting, trampling."—*The Times*, June 8, 1926.

great brown-winged orchis (*O. purpurea*) may be cited as an instance; and much commoner plants, such as the great butterfly orchis, suffer in the same way. One spring, for example, I came accidentally upon a large colony of these "butterflies," eighty or a hundred in number, on a waste piece of land at the foot of the Sussex Downs; a week later, passing that way again, I saw that hardly a blossom was left. In like manner you may see people going off with big bouquets of such scarce and beautiful flowers as the marsh gentian; and if you venture to expostulate, the reply will probably be: "Well, if *I* did not pick them, somebody else would"; which is quite true and equally irrelevant.

At another time it is the daffodils that are the attraction; and from two correspondents, one in East and the other in West Sussex, I have heard of the havoc that is wrought by marauding parties from the towns. "I saw a woman pass here recently," wrote one of my informants, "with six or seven bunches tied on her bicycle, each containing, I should say, about a hundred blooms." Such are the conditions, and such the "jocund company," in which Wordsworth's daffodils are now to be seen!

One of the rarest of British orchids is the Summer Ladies' Tresses, "the imminent extinction" of which is foreboded by a well-known Hampshire botanist. "The only spots in England for this very rare orchid were Wyre Forest, in Worcestershire, and the New Forest. From the former it had gone almost as soon as found, and the place in our forest, which twenty years ago was white with it, now will give but one or two spikes. But in 1900 it was found in another bog, not far off; and here, for some years, two hundred spikes might be counted, but now they have diminished to half a dozen. The cause of this deplorable loss was to be attributed to greedy or ignorant collecting."[1]

Indiscriminate plucking is, of course, less serious than uprooting, but nevertheless is a cause of the steady diminution of some delightful species. A friend of mind went to a chalk-pit in Sussex for a specimen or two of the bee orchis, but could see none. Meeting some boys, he questioned them about the missing flower, and received the cheering information: "We've got ninety-six."

[1]From a paper on "Wild Flowers of Hampshire," read at a meeting of the Southampton Gardeners' Society by Mr. J. F. Rayner, F.R.H.S., *Hants Advertiser*, September 17, 1927.

As for uprooting, to show what widespread ignorance or indifference there has long been on this point, a few examples will be sufficient. Here is a case, taken from the "Flora of Kent," in reference to the very rare Cyclamen:

> Towards the end of August, 1861, I was shown the native station of this plant......The people in those parts had found out it was in request, and had almost entirely extirpated it, digging up the roots and selling them for transplantation into shrubberies.

Nurserymen and owners of gardens are often offenders in this respect, and the process of abducting wild plants goes on in many places without hindrance and usually without protest. There is a wood in Surrey where the Martagon Lily grows wild; when I visited the spot I noticed a number of holes in the ground, testifying to the rapacity of those "knights of the trowel" who had lately been at work there. On the Shoreham shingles, until a few years ago, there grew ten or twelve fine clumps of wild seakale; then, one day, an inhabitant of a bungalow went out with a spade and coolly appropriated the lot. Such forays, as every flower-lover knows, are far from uncommon.[1]

Here again the mischief is of very ancient date, orchids and alpine plants being the chief sufferers. In Bingley's "A Tour in North Wales" (1798) we read how the Rev. W. Bingley himself, with another clergyman, the Rev. Peter Williams, made a successful ascent of one of the spurs of Snowdon, on an errand which has too often sent later marauders to the same locality. "We had along with us," he wrote, "a small basket to contain our provisions and hold the roots of such plants as we wished to transfer to his [the Rev. Peter's] garden"; and thus equipped they arrived at the top "in possession of all the plants we expected to find." This sort of thing has now been going on for over a century, and it is therefore not surprising that on Snowdon, as elsewhere, the rarer flowers are disappearing.

Nor is it our own land only that is thus overhauled. It may seem a slight matter at the present time, when the world has still so many unexplored regions, that wild foreign districts should be ransacked for the sake of the domestic garden. "Every one

[1]"That human interference is responsible for the decrease of the wild seakale there can be no doubt." — Dr. E. J. Salisbury.

loves flowers," says one of these bold adventurers;[1] "but how many people realize the forethought, knowledge, and care bestowed on them, the time and money — aye, and the risk to life and limb, which is paid gladly to maintain, and to increase, the stock of beauty in English gardens?" Still fewer persons, it may be surmised, realize to what this craze, if persevered in, must eventually lead — the world-wide sacrifice of the wildflower in the supposed interests of the tame, ending in the extension to foreign lands of the dearth which we are already beginning to experience in our own.

The hawker is another and very serious offender, and one against whom (being a poor man) wrath is more easily aroused. "During recent months," wrote Colonel Cuthbert James, M.P., in a letter to *The Times* in June, 1926, "I repeatedly have seen hawkers of the gipsy type peddling uprooted wildflowers from door to door — orchis, fritillary, cowslip, primrose, etc., in due season. It is, I submit, futile to appeal either to the aesthetic sense or good feelings of such persons, whose sole motive is pecuniary. Consequently some form of legislative enactment seems to be not only desirable, but actually necessary." That is very true; but what of the aesthetic sense or good feelings of the well-to-do persons who, by purchasing the plants, incite the hawkers to further acts of destruction?

The digging up of choice wild plants is already forbidden in some local by-laws, and ought to be more generally prohibited; but at present there is a lack of sufficiently strong public opinion to enforce legislation. Even as I write this, I see in a London paper[2] the odd suggestion that lovers of Nature may anticipate the spring-time by going out with a trowel and a basket, and removing from the crowded bank or hedgerow the roots of some familiar flowers which will flourish earlier and more luxuriantly in a garden; and then, when the season is over, the plants, improved by their change of soil, may be restored to their native habitat. Only common flowers are to be given this jaunt; but, even so, it is to be feared that, if the proposal were widely adopted, the *restoration* of the transplanted plants would too often be forgotten! Rare flowers never return. I have heard of several cases where the *Daphne Mezereum*, for example, has been carried into

[1]Captain F. Kingdon Ward, F.R.G.S., in "The Romance of Plant Hunting," 1924.
[2]The *Daily News*, February 3, 1926: "The Hedge Garden," by S. L. Bensusan.

captivity from its home in the woods to gratify the gardener's pleasure in so beautiful a flower; but I have yet to hear of a single instance of its being released, and it is becoming exceedingly scarce in certain Sussex plantations where it once was frequent. The trowel is a deadly instrument which ought never to be seen in the wilds.

But it is not only the thoughtless casual flower-lover, or the peddler employed by him, who is thus in fault; a not less dangerous enemy to our wildflowers is the "collector" — I hardly like to say the botanist, but really it is sometimes very difficult to draw the line. To a reasonable collecting no one would be disposed to make objection; but when it passes, as it often does, into "the mania of owning things," and when every one who calls himself a botanist must have his private herbarium, it becomes necessary to point out that the result is extremely injurious to our wild flowers. The establishment of "Exchange Clubs" causes rare plants to become rarer still, and far too many specimens are sometimes taken for such purposes. I note, for instance, in the Report of the Botanical Society and Exchange Club of the British Isles for 1926, the following comment by a well-known botanist in reference to the rare and lovely Marsh Gentian (*Gentiana Pneumonanthe*):

> Chobham Common, Surrey, August, 1926. Yes; but I am sorry to see this beautiful plant sent to Exchange Clubs from our county. It is becoming far too scarce.

It is a matter of regret that this plant, and others that might be named, should be so sent from *any* county, when there are good descriptions and illustrations which make identification quite easy. It appears from the Report that no fewer than 5,262 plants were thus "exchanged" in one year.

The evil of "collecting" is a very old one, which has been steadily on the increase for more than a hundred years. In a reference to the Lizard orchis, the following complaint was made as long ago as 1840 in Sowerby's "English Botany"[1]:

> It was formerly plentiful about Dartford, but a specimen is now of rare occurrence. Sir J. E. Smith lamented the cupidity of collectors of the past generation, but how much more evil is enacted

[1]Second Edition, 1840, vol. vii, p. 5.

by those of the present, some of whom, not content with gathering specimens for the herbarium, root up by thousands the gems and beauties of our national flora, not for the purposes of science, but of sordid gain.

Instances of this rapacity could easily be multiplied. Here is one, brief but eloquent, taken from Linton's "Flora of Derbyshire": "Lady's Slipper. Formerly abundant on the Heights of Abraham, but long since extirpated." In Mr. Reginald Farrer's book, "My Rock Garden," there is a fuller account of the extinction of this beautiful orchid in the Arncliffe valley:

> And worse is to follow; for a professor from the North — I will not unfold whether it were Edinburgh, Glasgow, or Aberdeen, or none of these, that produced this monster of men — put a price on the head of the Cypripedium, and offered the inhabitants so much for every rooted plant they sent him. The valley accordingly was swept bare, and until the patient plant was rediscovered last year (1907) there was nothing left to tell of the glen's ancient glory except one clump of the Cypripedium which, to keep it holy, had been removed to the vicarage garden, there to maintain in a mournful but secure isolation the bygone traditions of Arncliffe.

It seems that we must re-write Tennyson's "Flower in the Crannied Wall":

> "*Flower in the crannied wall,*
> *I pluck you out of the crannies.*"
> What self-convicted pilferer goes by,
> Filching the gems from Nature's coronal
> For storage in herbarium dusty-dry?
> A botanist, forsooth, the man is!
> But were it not correcter
> By some less reputable name to call
> That bane of things most lovely, the Collector?

The insane greed of collectors sometimes leads to situations which would be comical enough, were it not that the very existence of the flowers is at stake. Thus we read in Mr. F. Hamilton Davey's "Flora of Cornwall" a queer story of the fortunes of the Irish Butterwort in that county. Some specimens had been sent from Ireland to a Cornish botanist, who, fearing they would be lost during his temporary absence, "deposited them" in a secluded corner of a moor. When he returned and looked for the plants, he could not see them; but some years later the discovery was made that they had increased so greatly that they were to be counted in hundreds. Then, when the news spread, the collectors arrived from all quarters, and the butterworts were so nearly exterminated that the remnant had to be again transplanted!

The value of a herbarium is unquestioned; but, like other good things, even the herbarium may become an evil if it is not kept within due limits; in other words, if every man, woman, and child who is interested in rare flowers is going to press them for a collection, there will eventually be none left to press. The operations of the press-gang (for that term is quite justified in the circumstances) are already affecting certain plants very injuriously, and causing some botanists, who are sensible of the mischief that is being done, to turn to photography or painting — methods of preservation which, except for strictly scientific purposes, are much to be preferred to the mummifying process by which a plant is prepared for the collection.

Such, then, are some of the dangers with which the less common wildflowers have to contend in a struggle which is yearly becoming more difficult for them. I have mentioned only the avoidable danger; for, as I have said, the curtailment of our native flora as a consequence of the extension of building, cultivation, drainage of marshy lands, and so forth, falls under a different category, and must be reckoned as inevitable. Yet how serious it is, only those lovers of wildflowers who have themselves watched the process can be aware. All the more reason, therefore, that we should guard against any needless addition to such loss.

Of the strong attraction which wildflowers possess for many minds there can be no question — it is a fancy, a passion, which seizes not the young only, but equally the old; and numerous cases occur where the most unlikely persons (I have in mind a retired grocer who devoted his declining years to the pursuit) are strongly affected by it, sometimes to the surprise, or even the indignation, of relatives who cannot understand such profitless addiction to "weeds." And, by the irony of fate, it is this very interest in the flowers that now threatens to contribute to their ruin; for while their votaries have increased enormously in number during the past century, owing to the general growth of nature-studies, the flowers themselves have been on the decrease, with the prospect that, as years go on, the tragedy of the Lady's Slipper and other vanishing species may be repeated on a wider scale.

Mr. Baldwin was right. Wildflowers need sanctuary; and the first step towards obtaining it for them is to make known the increasing urgency of that need.

*Our Vanishing Wildflowers*

## The Need of Sanctuaries

Reference has been made in the preceding chapter to the etablishment of "Sanctuaries," where wanton injury to wild life would be prohibited. This would not benefit all flowers, for many grow in places which, being devoid of natural beauty, are unlikely to be included in such reservations; but, as the haunts of the rarer plants are frequently in the districts which specially claim defence, flower-lovers, like other nature-lovers, are necessarily interested in the success of the efforts that are being made to save all "beauty-spots" from destruction. That there is urgent need of protection for such places is obvious; for in the last ten or twelve years motors have opened a way to numberless secluded districts which were once safeguarded from injury by their own remoteness. This facility of access has often brought in its train the bungalow and the jerry-built cottage; and the more picturesque the place the greater, of course, is the likelihood of its being invaded and "developed."

I will first speak of mountain sanctuaries, not only because many of the rarest and choicest flowers are of Alpine habit, but because mountain scenery is at once the finest and the most easily spoiled. A good deal of attention has been directed to the injuries which are threatened, in pursuance of private or commercial interests, to upland districts and to various places of natural wildness in the Lake District, North Wales, and other parts of the kingdom, and it has become evident that, unless some concerted effort is made for resisting such acts of vandalism, the country will eventually suffer a loss which can never be repaired. Mark, for instance, the design — happily, as yet, no more than a design — of invading the Sty Head Pass, the very centre and citadel of the Cumbrian mountains, with a highway for motors; the havoc wrought in the Pass of Aberglaslyn, at Beddgelert, by railway works and tunnellings; and the disfigurement of the once shapely peak of Snowdon by the "summit hotel."

It is somewhat strange that, while Switzerland has its "Heimatschutz" (Homeland Preservation League), and while there is an English branch of the same, there is no similar organization in this country for the protection of our own scenery, though greater and greater encroachments are being made, year by year, on its remaining strongholds. All nature-lovers must applaud the effort to save the Alps from desecration; but to one who has before his eyes the ruin, not merely impending, but in actual course of accomplishment, of our own Welsh mountains, the thought will occur — does not charity, in the preservation of scenery as in other matters, begin at home?

The ultimate question must always be this: What is the essential character of mountain scenery? What is it that gives to mountains their unique value as a recreation ground for mind and body alike? Surely, above everything, it is their wildness, their aloofness from the din and turmoil of common life; and it follows that, if this solitude is so invaded as to be impaired or destroyed, the very feature which is the main attraction of the hills will have been lost. It is not visitation, but vulgarization, that is to be feared. If their sanctity is ruined, the mountains are mountains no more. Let visitors go to the heart of the hills on foot, and however great their numbers they need do the place no irreparable wrong. If they go on machines, panting and snorting up one side, and scorching furiously down the other, they will not only get no profit themselves, but they will ruin the very nature of the mountains for the generations that are to come.

To meet this increasing evil it is necessary not only to protest against any commercial schemes which would endanger public interests by doing damage to natural scenery of a high order, but further, as the only ultimate means of saving the characteristic features of our mountains and of other wild tracts, to advocate the nationalization of certain districts which are of unique value, by the establishment of public parks or "reservations," similar in kind to those already formed in America and elsewhere, in which the wild fauna and flora, together with all the natural beauties of the place, would be faithfully preserved. If such an organization were started, it might be posible in time so to widen its scope as to make it, like the Swiss "Heimatschutz," a guardian of whatever is beautiful throughout the land. Some such organized body of educated opinion is badly wanted, if the beauty of our villages and countryside, which constitutes one of the chief sources of happiness in our lives, is to be maintained.

It seems clear that lovers of beautiful scenery must not trust to these schemes of destruction lying long in abeyance, but must themselves act with energy. What is needed is an organization which will oppose every attack of the sort, and will give public warning when any of Nature's citadels are threatened. Had such a society existed in the past, the desecration of Snowdon might have been prevented. If no such society exists in the future, what has been done on Snowdon may yet be done on Scafell. There are, of course, commercial interests that have to be considered; but these ought not to over-ride the higher and more real interests which value mountains above mammon. The question, in brief, is not a local but a national one.

As with the mountains so, in due degree, with the plains, the heaths, the woods, the marshes, and the sea shores. The methods of protection may vary in different localities; the one important thing is that the conscience of the community should be awakened, and that some public action should be taken before it is too late. Some of their fairest scenery has already been lost, some little has been saved: if we wish to secure the rest we must shake off the delusion that such matters can always be happily settled by private contract between purchasers and owners; otherwise the result will be that, while a few spots are rescued, whole districts will be ruined, and then the lament will be not for our vanishing but for our vanished wildflowers.

Before this chapter closes it may be well that some reply should be made to those who see "selfishness" and "narrow-mindedness" in the protest against what is called the "opening up" of a wild piece of country. Let us accept by all means the maxim of "the greatest good of the greatest number," only we must be sure that what we seek is, in reality, the greatest good.

When it was proposed to kill the goose that laid the golden eggs, the opposition to the scheme was doubtless denounced as selfish and narrow-minded; yet the "opening up" of the goose was found in the end to have been a disaster. In like manner would the destruction of the natural and primitive condition of many hills and valleys be disastrous, for the simple reason that the very quality which now gives them a peculiar charm would then have disappeared. There is no selfishness in pointing out this fact; but, on the contrary, there is fatal folly in ignoring it.

*Our Vanishing Wildflowers*

It is in man's dealings with the mountains, where, owing to the untameable wildness of the scenery, any injury is certain to be irreparable, that the marks of the modern Vandal are most clearly seen.

*Seventy Years Among Savages*

### Slag-Heap or Sanctuary?

Mountains have in all ages given asylum to free races. Has the time come when a free race must give asylum to its mountains? If we are to have any voice in the answer, the question is one which, in this country at least, cannot much longer be set aside; for though the encroachments of "civilization" on wild Nature have been more or less discussed since the famous "Tours" of Thomas Pennant created the modern tourist, and sent him roaming through the hills, the problem of how to preserve our mountain scenery — if we wish to preserve it — has become much more pressing with the great industrial development of the past hundred years, and it is no exaggeration to say that if it is not solved within the next hundred years there may be no mountain scenery to preserve.

It is not to be doubted that, as civilization advances, mountain districts, like all other wild districts, must be gradually "opened out," and made to minister more fully to human wants; but, then, what *are* those wants, and how can they best be gratified? The man who owned the goose that laid the golden eggs wanted golden eggs, but his too hasty method of opening out the goose defeated the purpose he had in view. In like manner, if we want to make our mountains more serviceable to the people, we must think whether the methods which we are at present adopting will conduce to that end. Look at the working of these methods among the Cambrian and Cumbrian hills.

Snowdonia has long been a sufferer from foreign and native aggression. It is said that Edward I, to celebrate his conquest of Wales, held "a triumphal fair" on Snowdon, in open defiance of the national sentiment by which this peak was held as holy as was Parnassus by the Greeks. What is more surprising is that the Welsh themselves have in later times so fully acquiesced in the defilement of their sacred mountain, and that the present plight of Snowdon would seem to be a pride rather than a shame to them; for all earlier outrages sink into nothingness when compared with the work of the past twenty years. The copper-mines in Cwm Dyli, which have been worked, and neglected, and worked again, have greatly defaced the mountain, have poisoned the waters, and submerged the islands of Llyn Llydaw, once the haunt of the sea-gull; but it was not until the railway was built from Llanberis, and an hotel placed on the summit, that irreparable harm was done by deforming the natural shape of Y Wyddfa, the topmost peak, into a dull, blunted cone.

What is worse, the summit railway is to be followed by a network of electric railways round the base of the mountain, and the power for working these lines is to be procured by desecrating the very heart of Snowdon itself. Immense "works" have been erected at the foot of the waterfall (one of the finest in Wales) which descends from Llyn Llydaw into Nant Gwynant, and the lake is to be further enlarged in order that a greater force may be available. In a word, the most wild and beautiful mountain recess in Wales is being hopelessly ruined and vulgarized.

Then the railway will be constructed, and the larger valleys that lie round the skirts of Snowdon will be vulgarized also; indeed, the Pass of Aberglaslyn is already spoiled beyond redress. And for what object? Simply that private gain may be made out of public loss.

It is a curious fact, too, that this greed for exploiting the natural scenery of Wales goes hand in hand with a complete neglect of such legitimate and really useful means of utilizing the tourist season as the erection of signposts, and the maintenance of bridle-paths and mountain-tracks, which, without disfiguring the scenery, are of great service to walkers. There has been no attempt, apparently, for the past quarter of a century to keep these roads in repair, and even the path made in recent years by Sir Edward Watkin to the top of Snowdon, through Cwm Llan, is already blocked in several places by large boulders that have slipped on it.

Such is the latter state of this old Welsh mountain, of which it used to be said that "whoever slept upon Snowdon would wake inspired." The inspiration which to-day awaits those who wake upon Y Wyddfa is the sight of a rubbish-heap surmounted by a pot-house, with the usual appurtenances of civilization — post-office, railway-station, refreshment-rooms, cigar-ends, urinals, hordes of trippers, to whom the mountain means no more than the pier at Margate or the terrace at Windsor — almost everything that is civilized except a police-station, and who knows but even that may come? If there is still any "beauty born of murmuring sound" among the dwellers on Snowdon, it must be born of the slow-panting locomotive, or of the gurgling of whiskies in the hotel. And the view? In clear weather, we are told, it embraces the coast of Ireland. I have seen it embrace a line of "washing" hung out to dry on the edge of the Glaslyn precipice. This is what the Welsh "nonconformist conscience" has made of its holy hill.

In Cumberland, thanks to the efforts of a few faithful defenders and the powerful sentiment aroused by the Lake poets, there has been much less desecration, and the recent attempts of vandalism on these remaining strongholds of Nature have been mostly repulsed; indeed, it might be thought that the immediate danger in this quarter comes less from enemies than from overzealous friends, and that it is time a limit were put to the well-meant but mischievous practice of building memorial tablets in record either of personal associations or of fatal accidents. That the guide-books should tell us how Scott's "pilgrim of Nature" lost his life on Helvellyn, and how Matthew Arnold took a meditative walk there, is well enough; but to erect stones in memory of these events, and marble crosses on the various spots where rash cragsmen have fallen, seems rather indiscreet; for it is not fitting that a wild mountain should be plastered, like a lecture-hall or a cemetery, with epitaphs and inscriptions.

But it must not be supposed that Lakeland has not suffered even as Wales has done, though in a less degree, from the ravages of commercialism. Coniston is a sad proof of the contrary, where that once beautiful mountain, the Old Man, has been so ruined by the copper-mines that, as has been said of the gold-fields of Colorado, "the hills have been flayed of all their grass and scalped of all their timber; they are scarred and gashed and ulcerated all over from past mining operations — so ferociously does little man scratch at the breasts of his great calm mother when he thinks that jewels are there hidden."[1] I was told by Ruskin, whose windows at Brantwood looked westward across Coniston Water to the Old Man, that he thought the very sky above the mountain-top was poisoned and clouded by the mines.

Take the case of Thirlmere, too, that once wild and winding tarn, so narrow at the middle that it was spanned by a rustic bridge, but now enlarged into a Manchester water-tank. It is true that in this case — unlike the majority — a useful purpose was attained; but are we to believe that the *general* interests of the country are promoted by such feats of engineering? Some thirty years back I happened to be in Cumberland when a score or so of the city fathers of Manchester were prospecting for their water-supply, and it struck me that, though, municipally regarded, they were doubtless worthy of all praise, their personal appearance in that narrow valley, where, both on account of their mission and their portly figures, they bulked somewhat largely in the dalesmen's eyes, was decidedly incongruous; they reminded one, in fact, in their solid proportions, of what geologists call "erratic blocks," yet they did not fit quite so harmoniously into the upland scene. Such were the worthies who, as it was expressed, "improved" Thirlmere into what we now see it — a formless sheet of water, with a large dam at its lower end, some ornamental water-works on its banks, and a few submerged homesteads below its waves. No wonder that the coachmen who ply between Keswick and Grasmere are never weary of pointing out to the passengers these triumphs of human skill.

The desecration of our mountains is but part of the widespread

[1] James Thomson; letter from Central City, Colorado.

contempt for Nature and natural scenery which may be seen from end to end of the land; but it is among mountains, where Nature is at her wildest, that it strikes us the most. From what filthy-mindedness, we wonder, comes the strange conviction that a clear, swift stream is the right and proper receptacle for the rubbish of human homes? I know a Welsh village — the type, alas! of many villages in Wales and elsewhere — in which from the houses built on the steep bank of a pure mountain torrent there dribbles down into the river a tributary river of filth — dust, broken bottles, paper, old boots, decaying vegetables, and all kinds of refuse; and when the useful rats, attracted by the odour, try to act as scavengers, the authors of the nuisance post themselves behind the parapet of a neighbouring bridge to shoot the "vermin" with a gun!

Nor is it only on the natives of these districts that such reproach must fall; for, unhappily, the state of some of the well-known peaks and gullies, both in Wales and Cumberland, proves that many visitors also forget their duties to the hills. I have seen the famous Needle Gully, on the south flank of the Gable, literally lined with sandwich-papers and other mementoes of climbing parties, whose members would be ashamed to treat St. Paul's or Westminster Abbey with the like disrespect; and if the skilled cragsman can be guilty of such sacrilege, can we hope that the ordinary tripper will be more reverent in his ways?

Such acts are at least indications of a barbaric mood in the public mind, which, when expressed in the form of commercial enterprise, is capable of wreaking more damage on the mountains than a waterspout or an earthquake; and the question presents itself, Will this mood pass or be abated before a fatal mischief is done? For bad as things are now, there may be worse to follow. "Thank God," said Thoreau, "they cannot cut down the clouds." But can they not? With flying machines once perfected, will not the cloud, that "mountain o'er a mountain," share the fate of the hills? No mountain, assuredly, will escape. "As to the loftiest peaks of the Andes and Himalayas," says Reclus, "too high in the regions of cold for man to go to their summits, the day will come when he shall be able to reach them. Balloons have already carried him two or three thousand yards high; other aeronauts will bear and deposit him on Gaourisankar, as far as the 'great diadem of the dazzling heaven.'"

The danger lies not so much in the accessibility of cloud or mountain as in the reckless and irreverent spirit of the man who attains them. To soar to "the great diadem" is no harm; but if we turn the great diadem into a great muck-heap, shall we be the gainers by our flight?

Nor is it only the mountains that are being ruined by man's brutishness; the extinction of the wild life of the mountains is also threatened. It has to be remembered that these remote ranges are almost the only haunt where certain rare animals can still, to some extent, hold their own. Scarcely more than a hundred years ago the eagle was breeding in Borrowdale, as it still breeds in parts of the Scottish Highlands; and whether the present century shall witness the extermination of the buzzard, the kite, the peregrine, the raven, and other rare species, must depend partly on the protection afforded them by law against the sporting naturalist or "collector," mainly on the preservation of the mountains themselves from the capitalists' greed. Destructive birds, such as the eagle, must doubtless be doomed, but the wholesale disappearance of the greater birds, such as the buzzard, and of the more interesting mammals, such as the wild goat, would be a grievous loss to the nation. We have, therefore, to choose between such loss and the putting of some curb on the enterprise of the commercialist and the mania of the collector, for the mountain and its wild animals are one. Shall we ever have the wisdom to make each such district into an asylum for bird and mountain alike? At present the lover of wild Nature, himself somewhat of a *rara avis*, must be thankful for what is spared in his time; but it is his duty to think of the future also, and to avert, if he may do so, the ruin which he clearly foresees.

We come back, therefore, to the question whether we wish to hand on these mountains to our descendants as mountains or as something else. For if we allow our company-promoters to carve and tunnel the crags, to enlarge and discolour the lakes, to poison the streams, and to drive away the wild life from the hills, are we not once more killing the goose that laid the golden eggs? These hills of ours are small as compared with the great mountains of Europe, but they are as beautiful, and they are unique, and once ruined they cannot by any ingenuity be restored. It is true that Switzerland is employed in the same manner in spoiling the Jungfrau and Mont Blanc, but it must be remembered that Switzerland has a practically unlimited reserve of Alps, while we have but few mountains to spoil.[1] At present they are still something more than a playground for gymnasts, or a picnic-ground for tourists; they are mountains, a piece of unsophisticated wild Nature in our midst, and as such, their value, to those who know it, is beyond words. Let them still be a playground and a picnic-ground by all means, but under such conditions as will preserve their native features and their higher character. One would think that a nation which can spend hundreds of millions on a foreign war might afford to become the owner of its own mountains at home!

The pretence that there is something selfish and anti-democratic in the desire to save our mountain scenery from destruction is absurd; on the contrary, it is entirely owing to its devotion to the fetish of "property" that the public has so long allowed these places to be exploited for private gain, and has stood by in utter apathy and indifference while a handful of speculators and traders have benefited at the expense of the community. Nor do we give to our mountains even that protection which other antiquities enjoy. What would be said if a Bill were submitted and passed in Parliament to authorize some private company to pull Westminster Abbey or Stonehenge to pieces and make a profit out of the ruins? It is no exaggeration to say that the Society for the Preservation of Ancient Monuments, familiarly known as "Anti-Scrape," would have the whole nation at its back in its resistance to such vandalism; yet a mountain such as Snowdon is a far more ancient monument than Stonehenge or the Abbey, and the vandalism which is now being successfully accomplished is of a still more insensate kind.

It is a hollow fallacy, too, to suppose that it is "democratic" to fill up and destroy the rare silences and solitary spaces that a land may still possess, on the plea that they cannot be enjoyed by all. They *can* be enjoyed by all who are fitted to enjoy them, and the benefits that result from such enjoyment are in the long-run shared by all the nation alike. To make a railway to the top of a mountain such as Snowdon, and then to argue that it is a blessing to the weakly folk who could not otherwise get there,

---

[1]There is an English branch of the League for the Preservation of Swiss Scenery, which has the powerful support of *The Times* and other leading papers. Does not charity in this, as in other matters, begin at home?

is to overlook the fact that it is not to the cripples, but to the community, that the mountain belongs. "Whatsoever," says the communist Reclus, "may be the future of man, or the aspect of the world which he may create for himself, solitude, in that portion of Nature which is left free, will become more and more necessary to those men who wish to obtain renewed vigour of thought far from the conflict of opinions and voices. If the beautiful spots of the world should one day become a mere rendezvous for the worn and weary, they who love to live in the open air will have nothing left them but to take refuge in a bark on the midst of the waves. . . . Happily the mountain will always contain the sweetest places of retreat for him who flies from the beaten paths of fashion."

Wherein, then, lies the remedy for the dangers which I have described? Within the last few years there has been much rejoicing over the rescue of two or three estates in the Lake District, such as Catbells and Gowbarrow, from the clutch of the speculator, and all honour is certainly due to those by whom these victories were won; but it is evident that large sums of money cannot for ever be raised by private subscription to buy off the day of doom, and that while one favoured tract is being thus protected, another less fortunate one is being lost. We cannot save our mountains by these piecemeal purchases from the harpies who threaten them; such methods are too troublesome, too costly, too purely local to be successful in the main. There is only one thorough solution of the problem, and that is to *nationalize* such districts as Snowdonia, Lakeland, the Peak of Derbyshire, and other public holiday-haunts, and so to preserve them for the use and enjoyment of the people for all time. If parks, open spaces, railways, tramways, water, and other public needs can be municipalized, why not mountains? It is impossible to overestimate the value of mountains as a recreation-ground for soul and body, yet, while we are awaking to the need of maintaining public rights in other directions, we are allowing our mountains — in North Wales and elsewhere — to be sacrificed to commercial selfishness. If Snowdon, for instance, had been purchased by the public twenty years ago, the investment would have been a great deal more profitable than those in which we usually engage; but while we are willing to spend vast sums on grabbing other people's territory, we have not, of course, a penny to spare for the preservation of our own.

What we need, in short, is the appointment of mountain sanctuaries — highland parks, where the hills themselves, with the wild animals and plants whose life is of the hills, shall be preserved in their wildness as the cherished property of the people — consecrated places, where every one shall be entitled to walk, to climb, to rest, to meditate, to study Nature, to disport himself as he will, but *not* to injure or destroy. When we truly care for these hills of ours, we shall remove them from the tender mercies of the mine-owners and railway lords, who now seek profit in their disfigurement, and shall place them under a council of mountaineers and naturalists and nature lovers who understand and reverence them, with the instruction that they shall so administer their charge as to add to the present happiness and the permanent wealth of the nation. How long will it take us, hag-ridden as we are by the nightmare of private ownership, to awake to the necessity of such a change?

Pending that blessed time, I would point out to those public-spirited rich men (and we know there are such) who are ever looking for some useful outlet for their wealth, that here, in the shadow of this storm-cloud that overhangs our mountain scenery, they have a golden chance of ennobling themselves; for it is simple truth that the millionaire who should buy a Snowdon or a Scawfell, and make free gift of it to the people, would be a benefactor for all time, and would far outstrip in lasting philanthropy any donor of churches or charities, hospitals or libraries, scholarships or seats of learning. For mountains are the holiest ground that the heart of man has consecrated, and their educating influence is even more potent than that of books; they are the true authors, the standard works, printed in the most enduring type, that cheer and brace, as no written words can do, the minds of those who study them.

In what state, then, shall we hand on to those who follow us these sacred temples of Nature, which, as even so old-fashioned a writer as Wordsworth asserted, are "a sort of national property, in which every man has a right and interest who has an eye to perceive and a heart to enjoy"? The day cannot be far distant when our choice must be made, and it is between a sanctuary and a slag-heap that we must choose.

*On Cambrian and Cumbrian Hills*

# III
# SALT AS
# MAN OF LETTERS

In his biographies and critical studies, which make up a large part of his publications, Salt was most satisfied and successful when he treated authors with whom he had the most sympathy. . . .

George Hendrick, *Henry Salt*

### Shelley

During the latter half of the nineteenth century Shelley's influence was very powerful, not only upon the canons of poetry, but upon ideals of various kinds — upon free-thought, socialism, sex-questions, food-reform, and not a few other problems of intellectual and ethical import.

*Seventy Years Among Savages*

### Thoreau

A first reading of *Walden* was in my own case an epoch, a revelation. . . .

*Seventy Years Among Savages*

### Shaw

We were Shelleyans and Humanitarians. . . . My pastime has been writing sermons in plays, sermons preaching what Salt practised.

Shaw's "Preface" to *Salt and His Circle*

Shaw was, of course, the outstanding figure of Fabianism, as he was bound to be of any movement in which he took permanent part; but he was a great deal more than Fabian, he was humanitarian as well. . . .

*Seventy Years Among Savages*

\* \* \*

I have written books because I *liked* doing so, not because they brought me any profit.

*A Group of Unpublished Letters by Henry Salt to Joseph Ishill*

## *ON SHELLEY*

### *The Pioneer*

In claiming for Shelley the title of pioneer, it is necessary to show that his deliberately adopted principles have in very fact anticipated and influenced the opinions of succeeding generations, and that, so far from being a purblind visionary who occasionally stumbled on a truth, he was a genuine and clear-eyed prophet of religious and political freedom.

The enormous progress made by freethought during the years that have passed since Shelley's death would in itself be sufficient refutation, if any were needed, of the assertion that he wrecked his judgment and good fame by his deliberate adoption of "atheistic" principles. He was from first to last an "atheist" in the sense that he denied the existence of the personal deity of the theologians; though it is important to note that, as he himself says in the preface to *Laon and Cythna*, the object of his attack was "the erroneous and degrading idea which men have conceived of a Supreme Being, but not the Supreme Being itself" — it was not the presence, but the absence, of spirituality in the established creed that made Shelley an unbeliever.

I regard Shelley's early "atheism" and later "pantheism" as simply the negative and the affirmative sides of the same progressive but harmonious life-creed. In his earlier years his disposition was towards a vehement denial of a theology which he never ceased to detest; in his maturer years he made more frequent reference to the great World-Spirit in whom he had from the first believed. He grew wiser in the exercise of his religious faith, but the faith was the same throughout; there was progression, but no essential change.

For holding and publishing these views he was ostracised and insulted; and now the same views are held as a matter of course by a vast number, probably a majority, of earnest and thoughtful men, the only difference being that the colourless title "agnosticism" has been substituted for the more expressive word which Shelley, with characteristic ardour, "took up and wore as a gauntlet." . . .

It is generally recognised that two of the most momentous social problems which press for solution are the condition of the working classes and the emancipation of women; and it is a proof of the shrewdness of Shelley's instinct that he, alone among the poets of his era, strongly emphasised these two questions, anticipating in his conclusions the general principles, if not the particular methods, of the policy to which modern reformers incline.

It is true that, like Godwin, and indeed like all contemporary thinkers, with the possible exception of Robert Owen, he was unable to grasp the full significance, in its bearing on social questions, of the great industrial development which the introduction of machinery brought about: we cannot expect from Shelley an accurate knowledge of an economic change which in his time could be only very imperfectly understood. But that he had a singularly clear perception of the cardinal fact by which the relations of labour and capital are characterised — the fact that the poor workers support the lazy rich, and that industry is taxed for the maintenance of idleness — is obvious from many passages in his writings.

Here, for example, is a reference to the land question, which states the case with admirable incisiveness and vigour: "English reformers exclaim against sinecures, but the true pension-list is the rent-roll of the landed proprietors." And, again, of the extortions of the fund-holders, those *nouveaux riches* whose heartless vulgarity Shelley more than once condemns:

I put the thing in its simplest and most intelligible shape. The labourer, he that tills the ground and manufactures cloth, is the man who has to provide, out of what he would bring home to his wife and children, for the luxuries and comforts of those whose claims are represented by an annuity of forty-four millions a year levied upon the English nation.

Nor, while thus pointing out the actual dependence of the so-called independent classes, did he evade the consideration that he too, the scion of a wealthy house, was a debtor in like manner; he "shuddered to think" that the roof which covered him and the bed on which he slept were provided from the same source.

We see, therefore, that Shelley was well aware that pauperism is no sporadic, unaccountable phenomenon, but the necessary and logical counterpart of wealth, and that the footsteps of luxury are for ever dogged by the grim nemesis of destitution. . . .

Shelley's views on the sex question are too well known to need more than a brief reference; it is sufficient to point out that they are practically identical with those now held by the body of advanced thinkers. There is plenty of evidence in *Laon and Cythna* that he recognised and deplored the social subjection of woman, and the evil consequences that result therefrom to the other sex and to humanity in general. "Can man be free," he asks, "if woman be a slave?" And again:

> Woman!—She is his slave, she has become
> A thing I weep to speak—the child of scorn,
> The outcast of a desolated home.
> Falsehood and fear and toil, like waves, have worn
> Channels upon her cheek, which smiles adorn,
> As calm decks the false ocean; well ye know
> What Woman is, for none of Woman born
> Can choose but drain the bitter dregs of woe,
> Which ever from the oppressed to the oppressor flow.

The compulsion of the marriage-bond is explicitly condemned in the well-known *Notes to Queen Mab*, on the ground that, as the very essence of love is freedom of choice, society is not justified in imposing this restriction on the individual. That Shelley's views remained unchanged to the end may be gathered from the kindred, but maturer, passage of *Epipsychidion*:

> I never was attached to that great sect
> Whose doctrine is that each one should select
> Out of the crowd a mistress or a friend,
> And all the rest, though fair and wise, commend
> To cold oblivion—though 'tis in the code
> Of modern morals, and the beaten road
> Which those poor slaves with weary footsteps tread
> Who travel to their home among the dead
> By the broad highway of the world—and so
> With one chained friend, perhaps a jealous foe,
> The dreariest and the longest journey go.

As it is, the Shelleyan advocacy of free love has been much misrepresented, being often absurdly identified, whether through ignorance or prejudice, with a heartless libertinism to which it is utterly alien. The essence of Shelley's belief was that, unless human passion is to be brutalised and debased, the spiritual and higher elements of love must always be present; for this reason he condemned the stereotyped and loveless formula of marriage, but he did not stultify his own contention by sanctioning an equally dull and loveless sensuality. . . .

Now, other poets have sung, before and after, of humanity and brotherhood; but there is just this peculiarity about Shelley's method of handling these great themes. He does not, as so many writers have done, eulogise these virtues in the abstract, while shutting his eyes to the many wrongs inflicted on "the lower classes," which, albeit sanctioned by respectability and custom, render real brotherhood impossible — on the contrary, he goes to the heart of the matter, and denounces those evils which are the most deadly sources of cruelty and oppression. The true ruffian was to him (I quote his own words) "the respectable man — the smooth, smiling, polished villain, whom all the city honours; whose very trade is lies and murder; who buys his daily bread with the blood and tears of men."

In similar manner, when touching on our relations with "the lower animals," he did not, like a certain school of sentimentalists, prate of men's benevolent feelings towards the objects of their gluttony, and preach peace under conditions where peace does not exist; but boldly and consistently arraigned the prime cause

139

of animal suffering, the removal of which must precede the establishment of a genuine human sympathy with the lower races. Those who have knowledge of the recent progress of vegetarianism are aware that here too, in his condemnation of flesh-eating, Shelley was a precursor of a vital and growing reform. . . .

From *Percy Bysshe Shelley: Poet & Pionerr*

To me, Shelley has always appeared as one of those great poets who, like great mountains, if rightly viewed and approached, can give strength and comfort to mankind. The things which I love best of all in English poetry are Milton's *Lycidas*, that gem of perfect art, so rapturously beautiful to the ear, and certain passages and lyrics in Shelley's *Prometheus Unbound*, not less beautiful to the ear and still more beautiful to the heart.

*Company I Have Kept*

## ON THOREAU

. . . The most vigorous protest ever raised against that artificiality in life and literature which is one of the chief dangers of our complex civilisation, proceeded not from some sleepy old-world province, which might have been expected to be unable to keep pace with a progressive age, but from the heart of the busiest and most advanced nation on the globe — it is to Yankeeland that we owe the example and the teaching of the "Bachelor of Nature." The personality of Thoreau is so singular and so unique that it seems useless to attempt, as some have done, to draw out any elaborate parallel between his character and that of other social, or un-social, reformers, who have protested against some prevalent tendency in the age in which they lived. Those who are interested in seeking for literary prototypes may perhaps, in this case, find one in Abraham Cowley, a member of that school of gnomic poets with which Thoreau was so familiar, and moreover a zealous lover of the peace and solitude of nature. He lived in close retirement during the later years of his life, and his death, which, like Thoreau's, was due to a cold caught while he was botanising, is attributed by his biographer to "his very delight in the country and the fields, which he had long fancied above all other pleasures." Some of Cowley's remarks in his essays on solitude are conceived in a spirit very similar to that of Thoreau. "The First Minister of State," he says, "has not so much business in public as a wise man in private; if the one has little leisure to be alone, the other has less leisure to be in company; the one has but part of the affairs of one nation, the other all the works of God and nature under his consideration"; and elsewhere he expresses the wish that men could "unravel all they have woven, that we might have our woods and our innocence again, instead of our castles and our policies." But these parallels, between two men of widely different periods and purposes, can contain nothing more than slight and superficial resemblances. Nor, except for his general connection with Emerson and the transcendentalists, is it more easy to match Thoreau with any ethical writer of his own generation.

As a "poet-naturalist," however, Thoreau is distinctly akin to Richard Jefferies and other writers of that school. Jefferies' character was richer and more sensuous than Thoreau's, but they had the same mystic religious temperament, the same impatience of tradition and conventionality, the same passionate love of woods and fields and streams, and the same gift of brilliant language in which to record their observations. It is curious to compare these modern devotees of country life with the old-fashioned naturalists of whom Izaak Walton and Gilbert White are the most illustrious examples. While the honest old angler prattles on contentedly, like the babbling streams by which he spent his days, with here and there a pious reflection on the beneficence of Providence and the adaptation of means to ends, and while the kindly naturalist of Selborne devotes himself absolutely and unreservedly to the work of chronicling the fauna and flora of the district about which he writes, these later authors have brought to the treatment of similar subjects a far deeper insight into the beauty and pathos of nature, and a power of poetical description which was not dreamed of by their simple yet not less devoted predecessors. It is mainly to Thoreau in America, and to Jefferies in England, that we owe the recognition and study of what may be called the poetry of natural history — a style of thought and writing which is peculiar to the last thirty or forty years. The study of nature has, of course, been from time immemorial one of the great subjects of poetry, but, so far, it was nature in its more general aspects; it was not till comparatively recent years that there was discovered to be poetry also in the accurate and patient observation of natural phenomena. We have now learnt that natural history, which was formerly regarded as a grave and meritorious study of a distinctly prosaic kind, may be made to yield material for the most imaginative and poetical reflections.

When Thoreau died in 1862, Richard Jefferies was a boy of fourteen, busily engaged among his native Wiltshire Downs in laying the foundation of his wonderful knowledge of outdoor life. As far as I am aware, there is no mention of Thoreau in his writings, nor any indication that he had read him; yet one is often struck by suggestive resemblances in their manner of thought. Take, for instance, that half-serious, half-whimsical contention of Thoreau's, which has probably been more misunderstood than any other of his sayings — that Concord, in its natural features, contains all the phenomena that travellers have noted elsewhere — and compare it with the following opinion expressed by Jefferies: "It has long been one of my fancies that this country is an epitome of the natural world, and that if any one has come really into contact with its productions, and is familiar with them, and what they mean and represent, then he has a knowledge of all that exists on the earth." In reading these words, one has a difficulty in remembering that they were not written by Thoreau.

The association of Thoreau's name with the district in which he lived and died is likely to become closer and closer as the years go on. Great nature-lovers, it has been truly remarked, have the faculty of stamping the impress of their own character on whole regions of country, so that there are certain places which belong by supreme and indisputable right to certain persons who have made them peculiarly and perpetually their own. As the Lake District is inseparably connected with the names of the poets who dwelt and wrote there; as the Scotch border-land owns close allegiance to Scott, and the Ayrshire fields to Burns; and as the little Hampshire village of Selborne is the inalienable property of Gilbert White — so the thoughts of those who visit Concord turn inevitably to Thoreau. "Thoreau's affections and genius," says one of his admirers, "were so indissolubly bound up with this country that now he is gone he presents himself to my mind as one of these local genii or deified men whom the Scandinavian mythology gave as guardians to the northern coasts and mountains. These beings kept off murrain from the cattle and sickness from men. They made the nights sweet and salubrious, and the days productive. If Thoreau had lived in the early ages of Greece, he would have taken his place in the popular imagination along with his favourite god Pan."

That a personality so stubbornly and aggressively independent as Thoreau's would be a stumbling-block to many critics, good and bad alike, might have been foreseen, and indeed *was* foreseen, from the first. "What an easy task it would be," said one who understood him unusually well,[1] "for a lively and not

[1] John Weiss, *Christian Examiner*, July 1865.

entirely scrupulous pen to ridicule his notions, and raise such a cloud of ink in the clear medium as entirely to obscure his true and noble traits!'' Just three months after these prophetic words were written appeared Mr. Lowell's well-known criticism of Thoreau in the *North American Review*, afterwards reprinted in *My Study Windows*, an essay which was a masterpiece of hostile innuendo and ingenious misrepresentation, written with all the cleverness and brilliancy of which its author was capable. Mr. Lowell, who had been one of Thoreau's fellow-students at Harvard University, and had held friendly relations with him after the close of their college career, had certainly not made the discovery of his intellectual feebleness at the time of the publication of the *Week on the Concord River* in 1849, for in that same year he highly eulogised him in the *Massachusetts Quarterly* as one of those rare persons who, in a utilitarian age, can still feel and express the almost indefinable charm of wild nature, and further spoke of him in a tone of much personal friendliness. Ten years later, however, this friendly acquaintance was sharply terminated by a difference which arose, as already mentioned, about an article contributed by Thoreau to the *Atlantic Monthly*, then under Mr. Lowell's editorship; and we have had it stated, on Emerson's authority, that Mr. Lowell ''never forgave Thoreau for having wounded his self-consciousness'' — presumably in a correspondence that arose on this subject. I make no apology for calling attention to this nexus of events, because it furnishes the explanation of the otherwise strange animus which underlies Lowell's article. Brilliant as is the view obtained from *My Study Windows*, it ought to be more generally known that there is at least one pane therein which is discoloured and distorted, and which cannot be trusted by those literary students who would keep an unprejudiced outlook.

"A skulker" is the phrase in which Mr. R. L. Stevenson summed up Thoreau's character in his essay in *Men and Books*; but as he himself admits in the later-written preface that he had quite misread Thoreau through lack of sufficient knowledge of his life, there is no reason why admirers of *Walden* should feel disturbed at the bestowal of that singularly inappropriate epithet. Other critics, again, while enjoying much of Thoreau's writing, have been haunted by a suspicion that he was the victim of a theatrical self-consciousness, and that he became a hermit rather to attract attention than to avoid it. "We have a mistrust of the sincerity of the St. Simeon Stylites," said a contemporary reviewer of *Walden*, "and suspect that they come down from the pillars in the night-time when nobody is looking at them. Diogenes placed his tub where Alexander would be sure of seeing it, and Mr. Thoreau ingenuously confesses that he went out to dine." So inconceivable does it seem to those who have not considered, much less practised, a simple and frugal life, that a man should deliberately and for his own pleasure, abandon what *they* believe to be luxuries and comforts, that critics are always discovering some far-fetched and non-existent object in the Walden experiment, while they miss its true and salutary lessons.

It seems scarcely necessary nowadays to rebut the absurd charge of "selfishness" which used once to be brought against Thoreau. But the charge still crops up now and then in belated circles of thought. "The general impression of the reader," says the *Church Quarterly Review*,[1] "is that, while the descriptions of scenery are extremely beautiful, and the notes about animal life and plants are most interesting, yet the man himself is thoroughly selfish, quite out of sympathy with men and their sufferings, barbaric, if not animal, in his tastes, and needlessly profane."

Thoreau's "lack of ambition" is another point that has caused him to be much misunderstood — even Emerson gave his sanction to this rather futile complaint. "I cannot help counting it a fault in him," he said, "that he had no ambition. Wanting this, instead of engineering for all America, he was the captain of a huckleberry party. Pounding beans is good to the end of pounding empires one of these days; but if, at the end of years, it is still only beans!" But the obvious answer to this criticism is that, in Thoreau's case, it was *not* only beans. The chapter on "The Bean Field," in *Walden*, is one of the most imaginative and mystic in all his works — "it was no longer beans that I hoed," he says, "nor I that hoed beans" — for the object of his quest and labour was not the actual huckleberry nor the tangible bean, but the glorified and idealised fruit of a lifetime spent in communion with nature, which imparted to his writings a freshness and fragrance as of nature itself. In this matter Thorea was the wiser judge of his own powers, and conferred a far greater benefit on the human race by writing *Walden* than he could have done by engineering for all America.

[1]October 1895.

After all that has been said in this book of Thoreau's great debt to Emerson, it may, I think, be added without prejudice or ingratitude that the common misapprehension of Thoreau's character must be partly traced back to Emerson's "Biographical Sketch," and to his unfortunate manner of editing the Letters and Poems. That excessive insistence on Thoreau's "stoicism," to the subordination of his gentler and more affectionate traits, has done much to postpone a general recognition of the deep tenderness that underlay the rugged nature and rough sayings of the author of *Walden*. It is said that as Thoreau's character matured and hardened, his friendship with Emerson grew somewhat "Roman" and austere; and we may be permitted to doubt whether Emerson had really gauged his friend's mind as fully as he imagined. That Thoreau, on his side, was sensible of Emerson's limitations, is proved by the opinion which he expressed to a friend that Emerson would be classed by posterity with Sir Thomas Browne — an estimate far lower than the usual one.

And here I would hazard the suggestion (though well aware that it must at present seem fantastic) that Thoreau's genius will eventually be at least as highly valued as Emerson's. No sane critic could for a moment doubt the mighty influence which Emerson's great and beneficent intellect wielded among his contemporaries, or dream of comparing Thoreau with him as a nineteenth-century power. But the class of mind which has the most lasting hold on men's interest and homage is not always, and not often, the same as that which rules contemporary thought; and in the long run the race is to the most brilliant rather than to the most balanced of writers, to the poet rather than to the philosopher, to him who most keenly challenges the curiosity and imagination of his readers. Of all the Concord group, by far the most inspired, stimulating, and vital personality is Thoreau's; and when time has softened down the friction caused by superficial blemishes and misunderstandings, the world will realise that it was no mere Emersonian disciple, but a master-mind and heart of hearts who left that burning message to his fellow-men.

The sum of the whole matter is, that Thoreau had a clear and definite object before him which he followed with inflexible earnestness, and that his very faults and oddities subserved the main purpose of his life. "There is a providence in his writings," says John Weiss, "which ought to protect him from the complaint that he was not somebody else. No man ever lived who paid more ardent and unselfish attention to his business. If pure minds are sent into the world upon errands, with strict injunction not to stray by other paths, Thoreau certainly was one of these elect. A great deal of criticism is inspired by the inability to perceive the function and predestined quality of the man who passes in review. It only succeeds in explaining the difference between him and the critic. Such a decided fact as a man of genius is, ought to be gratefully accepted and interpreted.''

That Thoreau's doctrines, no less than his character, have their shortcomings and imperfections, few will be disposed to deny. He could not realise, or perhaps did not care to realise, the immense scope and complexity of the whole social problem; he had scarcely the data or opportunities for doing so; and in any case his intensely individualistic nature would probably have incapacitated him. We therefore cannot look to him for any full and satisfactory solution of the difficulties by which our modern civilisation is surrounded, but it would be a great error to conclude that we are not to look to him at all. If it is true that the deadlock resulting from the antagonism of labour and capital can never be relieved without external legislation, it is equally true that there can be no real regeneration of society without the self-improvement of the individual man; it is idle to assert that the one or the other must come first — *both* are necessary, and the two must be carried on side by side. In Thoreau the social instinct was deficient or undeveloped; but, on the other hand, he has set forth the gospel of the higher intellectual individualism with more force and ability than any modern writer; if it be but a half-truth that he preaches, it is none the less a half-truth of the utmost moment and significance. "As to Thoreau," says Edward Carpenter, in *England's Ideal*, a volume worthy to rank with *Walden* in the literature of plain living and high thinking, "the real truth about him is that he was a thorough economist. He reduced life to its simplest terms, and having, so to speak, labour in his right hand and its reward in his left, he had no difficulty in seeing what was worth labouring for and what was not, and no hesitation in discarding things which he did not think *worth* the time or trouble of production.''

We have seen that he was not, like Emerson, a philosopher of wide far-reaching sympathies and cautious judicial temperament, but rather a prophet and monitor — outspoken, unsparing, irreconcilable. He addressed himself to the correction of certain popular tendencies which he perceived to be mischievous and delusive, and preached what may be comprehensively termed a gospel of simplicity, in direct antagonism to the prevailing tone of a self-indulgent and artificial society. Who will venture to say that the protest was not needed then — that it is not still more needed now? "The years which have passed," says a well-known writer,[1] "since Thoreau came back out of Walden wood, to attend to his father's business of pencil-making, have added more than the previous century to the trappings and baggage of social life, which he held, and taught by precept and example, that men would be both better and happier for doing without. And while we succumb and fall year by year more under the dominion of these trappings, and life gets more and more overlaid with one kind and another of upholsteries, the idea of something simpler and nobler probably never haunted men's minds more than at this time." Herein lies the strength of Thoreau's position, that the very excess of the evil, which turns our supposed comforts into discomforts and our luxuries into burdens, must at last induce us to listen to the voice of sobriety and reason.

As to the manner in which Thoreau expresses his convictions nothing more need here be said, except that his style is justly adapted to his sentiments. His "knock-down blows at current opinion" are likened by Mr. R. L. Stevenson to the "posers" of a child, "which leave the orthodox in a kind of speechless agony." "They know the thing is nonsense — they are sure there must be an answer, yet somehow they cannot find it." We may shrewdly doubt whether the conclusive answer will ever be forthcoming; but it is something that people should be at all aroused from the complacent lethargy of custom and tradition. Thoreau is thus seen to have a quickening, stimulating, and, at times, exasperating effect as an ethical teacher; it is no part of his object to prophesy smooth things, to deal tenderly with the weaknesses of his readers, or even to explain those features of his doctrine which, from their novelty or unpopularity, are most likely to be misunderstood. This being so, his character and writings were certain to prove as distasteful to some readers as they are attractive to others; if he is a good deal misapplied at present, time will set that right.

[1] Mr. T. Hughes, *Academy*, 17th November 1877.

In conclusion, we see in Thoreau the extraordinary product of an extraordinary era — his strange, self-centred, solitary figure, unique in the annals of literature, challenges attention by its originality, audacity, and independence. He had, it has been well remarked, "a constitutional *No* in him"; he renounced much that other men held dear, and set his heart on objects which to the world seemed valueless; it was part of his mission to question, to deny, to contradict. But his genius was not only of the negative and destructive order. In an age when not one man in a thousand had a real sympathy with nature, he attained to an almost miraculous acquaintance with her most cherished secrets; in an age of pessimism, when most men, as he himself expresses it, "lead lives of quiet desperation," he was filled with an absolute confidence in the justice and benevolence of his destiny; in an age of artificial complexity, when the ideal is unduly divorced from the practical, and society stands in false antagonism to nature, he, a devout pantheist, saw everywhere simplicity, oneness, relationship. In his view, God was not to be considered apart from the material world, nor was man to be set above and aloof from the rest of creation and the lower forms of life; he tracked everywhere the same divine intelligence — "inanimate" nature there was none, since all was instinct with the same universal spirit. It was his purpose, in a word, "to civilise nature with the highest intuitions of the mind, which show her simplicity to restless and artificial men."

This ideal he pursued, as we have seen, with a rare courage, sincerity, and self-devotion. Whether he succeeded or failed in his endeavour is a question which time alone can fully answer. His example and doctrines were coldly and incredulously received during his lifetime by most of those with whom he came in contact, and his comparatively early death cut him off, in the prime of his vigour, from reaping the harvest he had sown with such patience and assiduity; so far his career, like that of most idealists, must be confessed a failure. But these are not the tests by which idealists, least of all Thoreau, can be judged. For he enjoyed, in the first place, that priceless and inalienable success which consists in perfect serenity of mind and contentment with one's own fortunes. "If the day and night," he says in *Walden*, "are such that you greet them with joy, and life emits a fragrance like flowers and sweet-scented herbs — is more elastic, starry, and immortal — that is your success." And, secondly, he had the assurance, which is seldom denied to a great man, that the true value of his work would ultimately be recognised and appreciated. During the period that has passed since his death his fame has steadily increased both in America and England, and is destined to increase yet further.

The blemishes and mannerisms of Thoreau's character are written on its surface, easy to be read by the indifferent passer-by who may miss the strong and sterling faculties that underlie them. His lack of geniality, his rusticity, his occasional littleness of tone and temper, his impatience of custom, degenerating sometimes into injustice, his too sensitive self-consciousness, his trick of over-statement in the expression of his views — these were incidental failings which did not mar the essential nobility of his nature. We shall do wisely in taking him just as he is, neither shutting our eyes to his defects nor greatly deploring their existence, but remembering that in so genuine and distinctive an individuality the "faults" have their due place and proportion no less than the "virtues." Had he added the merits he lacked to those which he possessed, had he combined the social with the individual qualities, had he been more catholic in his philosophy and more guarded in his expression, then we might indeed have admired him more, but should scarcely have loved him so well, for his character, whatever it gained in fulness, would have missed the peculiar freshness and piquancy which are now its chief attrac-tion — whatever else he might have been, he would not have been Thoreau.

*Life of Thoreau* (1896)

### *"One World at a Time"*

To foolish questioners, the sort
    That tranquil deathbeds oft hath vexed,
Asking, "As this world's hours draw short,
    Art ready, friend, to face the next?",
Was never yet returned reply
    More simple, yet in truth sublime,
By brave men doubting not to die,
    Than Thoreau's: "One world at a time".

*Cum Grano*

## ON RICHARD JEFFERIES

How greatly it can retard the reputation of a nature-writer, to be suspected of having designs on the intelligence of his readers, may be seen from the parallel case of Richard Jefferies, who in his earlier period was a naturalist, a poet-naturalist in his maturity. Why was it that so essentially second-rate a book as Jefferies's *Gamekeeper at Home* was popular and successful, while the wonderful *Story of my Heart* had to be sold off at sixpence a copy? Simply because the *Story* was weighted with subversive "ideas," while the *Gamekeeper* was pleasantly devoid of any such perilous cargo. It is probable that had all Jefferies's works been on the same lines as his *Story*, his name would be far less known than it is to-day.

*Company I Have Kept*


. . . If ever there was an inspired work, a real book of prophecy, such a one is Jefferies's *Story of my Heart*, in which, with his gaze fixed on a future society, where the term *pauper* ("inexpressibly wicked word") shall be unknown, he speaks in scathing condemnation of the present lack of just and equitable distribution, which keeps the bulk of the human race still labouring for bare sustenance and shelter.

In a study of Jefferies's life and ideals, published in 1894, I drew attention to the marked change that came over his views, during his later years, on social and religious questions, a ripening of thought, accompanied by a corresponding growth of literary style, which can be measured by the great superiority of *The Story* over such books as *The Gamekeeper at Home*; and in connection with this subject I pointed out that the incident recorded by Sir Walter

Besant in his *Eulogy of Richard Jefferies* of a death-bed return to the Christian faith, at a time when Jefferies was physically and intellectually a wreck, could not be accepted as in any way reversing the authoritative statement of his religious convictions which he had himself published in his *Story*. For this I was taken to task in several papers as having perverted biography in the interest of my own prejudiced opinions; but under this censure, not to mention that my views were shared by those friends and students of Jefferies with whom I was brought in touch, I had one unsuspected source of consolation in the fact that Sir Walter Besant told me in private correspondence that, from what he had learnt since the publication of his *Eulogy*, he was convinced that I was quite right. I did not make this public until many years later, when a new edition of my book appeared: there was then some further outcry in a section of the press; but this was not repeated when Mr. Edward Thomas, in the latest and fullest biography of Jefferies, dismissed the supposed conversion as a wrong interpretation by "narrow sectarians" who ignored the work of Jefferies's maturity.

*Seventy Years Among Savages*

I have never regretted my part in that controversy. But I am well aware that it is not as socialist or rationalist that Jefferies will be remembered, but as the poet-naturalist who wrote some very beautiful books.

*Company I Have Kept*

## ON EDWARD CARPENTER

### To Edward Carpenter
### in Ceylon (1891)

O'er Ceylon's isle the spicy breezes
Blow soft, while torpid Britain freezes.
Say, Bard of Brotherhood, is't fair?
We shivering here, you basking there?
Is this your "Towards Democracy"?
Are we your freeborn comrades—we,
Left wandering thus, like spirits lost,
In purgatorial fog and frost,
While you sit calm, 'neath summer skies,
On Adam's Peak in Adam's guise?

*Cum Grano*

Carpenter is usually, and correctly, spoken of as a reformer and idealist; but to the deeper student the faculty which specially distinguished him is what may be called his mysticism or seership, the sense of a serene and illuminative wisdom which is felt through his written word. No understanding reader of certain poems in *Towards Democracy*, or of the four wonderful chapters in *From Adam's Peak to Elephanta*, entitled "A Visit to a Gnani," will fail to see that he combined in himself the profound repose of Oriental thought with the reforming activity of the West; he was at once occultist and publicist, dreamer and reformer. Moreover, to the free, spacious love of brotherhood, of which Whitman was the spokesman, he added something of Thoreau's intenser passion for simplicity; he was at once the Thoreau and the Whitman of the English democratic movement. To those who have not yet made acquaintance with his writings, I would say, begin with the two volumes on social questions, *England's Ideal*, and *Civilisation, Its Cause and Cure*, which contain the less abstruse portion of his philosophy and constitute the best exposition of that "Return to Nature" advocated by Rousseau, Shelley, Tolstoy, and other humane thinkers.

*Company I Have Kept*

## *ON DE QUINCEY*

To Messrs. Bell's *Miniature Series of Great Writers* I contributed a little book on De Quincey, designed to show that together with his high gift of imagination and great literary powers, he was endowed with a sensibility far in advance not only of his own age, but of that in which such confident censure was passed on "the opium eater". The book (now out of print) had the misfortune to appear, if not on Christmas Eve, on a date not very distant from it, and accordingly, as far as any press-notice was concerned, practically disappeared from human ken as soon as it was published.

. . . we know, on his own authority, that the subject of opium was only subsidiary to his main purpose, which was "to reveal something of the grandeur which belongs potentially to human dreams"; it was the faculty of dreaming, not the powers of opium, by which his work was inspired; and therefore he lavished on the description of those dreams all the wealth of his "impassioned prose" which has made the *Confessions* one of the masterpieces of English literature. . . .

*Company I Have Kept*

Were it not a common practice of reviewers, in estimating the work of a great writer, to omit, as far as possible, any mention of humane sympathies shown by him, it would be strange that De Quincey should be represented as a mere "dreamer" and visionary; for in truth, in spite of the transcendental Toryism of his politics, he was in several respects a pioneer of advanced humanitarian thought, especially in the question of corporal punishment, on which he spoke, a hundred years ago, with a dignity and foresight which might put to shame many purblind "progressives" of to-day. His profound regard for a suffering humanity is one of the noblest features in his writings; he rejoiced, for instance, at the interference of Parliament to amend the "ruinous social evil" of female labour in mines; and he spoke of the cruelty of that spirit which could look "lightly and indulgently on the affecting spectacle of female prostitution." "All

I have ever had enjoyment of in life," he said, "seems to rise up to reproach me for my happiness, when I see such misery, and think there is so much of it in the world." It is amusing to read animadversions on De Quincey's "lack of moral fibre," written by critics who lag more than a century behind him in some of the matters that afford an unequivocal test of man's advance from barbarism to civilization.

*Seventy Years Among Savages*

## ON JAMES THOMSON ("B.V.")

So wonderful a poem as *The City of Dreadful Night* needs no apology; its justification is in its own grandeur and strength: nor ought such literature to be depressing in its effect on the reader's mind, but rather (in its right sphere and relation) a means of enlightenment and help. For whatever the subject and moral of a poem may be, there is nothing saddening in Art, provided the form and treatment be adequate; we are not discouraged but cheered by any revelation of feeling that is sincerely and nobly expressed. I hold Thomson, therefore, pessimist though he was, to have been, by virtue of his indomitable courage and love of truth, one of the inspired voices of democracy.

*Seventy Years Among Savages*

When we take into consideration Thomson's whole body of work, poetry and prose together, it must in justice be said that he possesses the two prime qualities that are essential to the making of a great writer. In the first place, he has that strong sense of humanity which lies at the back of all really memorable literature; pessimist though he may be, his sympathies are entirely human; the subject, in one shape or another, of all his writings is that great struggle between Love and Death, the pessimistic view of which must present itself, in certain moods and at certain times, to the mind of every thoughtful person. Secondly, he is gifted

155

with the not less indispensable faculty of poetic and artistic expression — the rich tone, the massive strength, the subtle melody of his language will scarcely be denied by those who have made it their study. Popular he perhaps can never be, in the ordinary sense, since his doctrines all point to a conclusion disagreeable to the popular taste; but when once his claim to immortality is impartially considered, it will be impossible to deny that his position in English literature is unique; a special niche will have to be set apart for him in the gallery of poets.

*The Life of James Thomson ("B.V.")*

## ON TENNYSON

"Scarcely any other artist in verse of the same rank has ever lived on such scanty revenues of thought as Tennyson. While it cannot be pretended that he is a great sculptor, he is certainly an exquisite carver of luxuries in ivory; but we must be content to admire the caskets, for there are no jewels inside. His meditation at the best is that of a good leading-article; he is a pensioner on the thought of his age. His nerves are so weak that any largish event — a Crimean war, or a Volunteer movement — sets him off in hysterics. Nothing gives one a keener insight into the want of robustness in the educated English intellect of the age, than the fact that nine-tenths of our best known literary men look upon him as a profound philosopher. A great school of the poets is dying out: it will die decently, elegantly, in the full odour of respectability, with our Laureate."

So wrote James Thomson, in an essay published some twenty-seven years ago; and it is interesting at the present time, when the death of Tennyson is being followed in due course by his deification, to observe the shrewdness of the criticism. . . .

Let us all be grateful to Lord Tennyson and his followers for the gifts they had to give us — for the charm of idyllic beauty, and the repose of faultless style — but it was of sterner stuff that the great poets were made who preceded them in the world of letters, and it is of sterner stuff that the poets of the future must be made, who shall approve themselves the true literary successors of Wordsworth and Byron and Shelley.

. . . As in the case of Shelley, so in the case of Tennyson, I submit that the philosophy which underlies the poetry, must be studied — candidly studied — together with the poetry itself, before a correct opinion can be formed of either. Thus examined, Lord Tennyson's social philosophy is found to be that of a man who, by the conditions of his birth, education, temperament, and general surroundings, was quite incapacitated for recognising the progressive and intellectual tendencies of the times in which he lived.

*Tennyson as A Thinker*

## ON TRANSLATING VIRGIL

Ties that are earliest formed usually last longest; and so it is that in many minds the love of the classics is very strongly entrenched in old age. In my case it was Virgil who had especially charmed me in boyhood; and to try to translate portions of the Georgics into English verse used to be one of my recreations before I had left school. Then, in later life, there were certain passages in Ovid that tempted a vegetarian to try his hand on them; and Martial's epigrams were a constant delight, for no one who was an interested student of Queer Fish could fail to be allured by the writer who, of all the ancients, was the keenest observer of the humorous aspects of social life. Under the title of "The Father of Epigram", some of my verse translations from Martial were published by Mr. Ramsay MacDonald in his *Socialist Review*.

But it was with selections from Lucretius that I first ventured before the public in book form, and owing to the encouragement then received proceeded to Virgil. In the *Treasures of Lucretius*, I adopted, as the handiest form for translation, what I called, with a hardihood which still surprises me, an irregular sequence of rhymed lines "as in Milton's *Lycidas*". I say hardihood; for seeing that *Lycidas* is one of the most perfect poems ever written, it must appear somewhat audacious on the part of a mere interpreter even to name that poem as his pattern; but the fact of *Lycidas* being so universally known was at once my reason and my excuse. This substitute for the hitherto commonly used forms — the heroic couplet, or the blank verse — which for different reasons seemed to me to have been failures, I carried on to my Virgilian attempts.

I say "attempts", because of course I was well aware that actual success is impossible: what impels a translator of Virgil, or of any other great poet, is his love for the original, and a desire to express it in his own language as far as it can be there expressed. It was thus that, armed with such experience as I had acquired from my venture with Lucretius, I printed, four years ago, under the title of *The Story of Dido and AEneas*, a version of the famous fourth Book of Virgil's AEneid, in the preface to which I repeated and enlarged what I had said about the *Lycidas* as a model, the free irregular sequence of rhymed iambic lines. . . .

I was able, when I published a version of the whole AEneid two years later, to avoid certain errors and defects which might otherwise have been uncorrected. . . .

On one matter, whatever the critics may say, I am quite impenitent; and that is my assertion that Virgil, not Homer, is the great poet of antiquity. I said in my preface, and I repeat with assurance, that the final test in art is not originality but achievement, and in all the qualities that mark the highest order of poetry Virgil greatly excels his predecessor and (if you like) his master. . . . Into what perfect thing Virgil could make an old legend may be seen in the fourth AEneid, when he tells the story of Dido, and in the sixth, the descent to Hades. It would be interesting to know where, in ancient literature, there is anything to match either of those great masterpieces of art.

*Company I Have Kept*

## *MEMORIES OF ETON*

In some reminiscences, *Eton under Hornby,* published in 1910, I gave a description of the public-school education of fifty years ago, a system probably not much worse than that of to-day; and the conclusion reached was that as Eton never really changes, it is best to regard her, as she regards other institutions, in a mood of good-natured unconcern, and as a subject less for argument than for anecdote. Eton has been pre-eminently the school "where ignorance is bliss," and in a much wider sense than that intended by the poet Gray in his famous ode "On a Distant Prospect of Eton College." For, if it be true of schoolboys that "thought would destroy their paradise" — that is, the thought merely of the personal ailments of mature age — how much more disturbing would be the contemplation of the vast social wrongs that fill the world with suffering! Of such sombre thought Eton knew nothing, but basked content in the warmth of her own supreme self-satisfaction; and the Eton life was probably the most enjoyable of all hitherto invented forms of heedless existence.

*Seventy Years Among Savages*

It was felt to be the beginning of a new epoch at Eton when Dr. Hornby succeeded Dr. Balston in the headmastership; and certainly the contrast between the two men was as striking as that between the two principles which they were supposed to represent — the old and the new method of education.

159

Dr. Balston was the very ideal of the majestic and unbending Toryism hitherto dominant; he had a personality which was felt throughout the school, and he was himself a model of unswerving devotion to an immemorial routine. It was whispered, indeed, that he *slept* in cap and gown, so rarely did he relax his severities of dress and demeanour; and so great was the awe inspired by his stately appearance that a slight stammer in his speech, which in some headmasters might have detracted from their authority, was in his case the means rather of enhancing it. He had a habit, when dismissing a boy from his presence, of telling him (with a rippling quaver on the words) to ''run away, run away, run away'' — as if he felt that, when released from the ordeal of such an interview, the natural gaiety of boyhood might be permitted to re-assert itself; and it is said that on one occasion, when he had been speaking to a famous athlete named Tinné, a young man — boy he could hardly be called — of Herculean proportions and of corresponding dignity, he was overheard to give him the same parting injunction, ''Run away, run away, run away, Tinné'' — as if bidding an infant toddle off to its hoop or marbles.

Dr. Hornby was the very reverse of all this. Appointed as a reformer, he was as inferior to his predecessor in all matters of routine as he was superior to him in initiative; and instead of making himself a familiar figure, as Balston had done, in every part of Eton, he seemed to live almost the life of a recluse, spending much of his time at Black Potts, a riverside villa, beyond the limit of the Eton Playing Fields; . . .

The general feeling about Dr. Hornby among the boys themselves was that he was too considerate as a man to be quite successful as a master. . . .

A strict moralist, Dr. Hornby's morals were simply of the old-fashioned order; and he was never really accessible to modern ideas. When it was first proposed to place a bust of Shelley in the Upper School (where it now stands), he is said to have replied, ''No; he was a bad man,'' and to have expressed his humorous regret that the poet had not been educated at Harrow.

*Eton Under Hornby*

## ON SHAW

It must have been in the year 1880, or thereabouts, that my brother-in-law, J. L. Joynes, who was closely connected with the Social Democratic Federation, brought the news to Eton, where I was then an assistant master, that he had made the acquaintance in London of a very clever and amusing Irishman named Shaw, and proposed that he should bring him down some week-end on a visit. He did so, and introduced to us a tall, thin young man whose black coat, and somewhat staid, almost penurious appearance, were remembered by us afterwards from their contrast with the exuberant Jaeger suits that distinguished the G.B.S. of the nineties. Of his cleverness there could be no doubt.

From this meeting an intimate friendship resulted; and from the time when we left Eton, at the end of 1884, for some fourteen years we saw him very often. He said at a later date that it was "the Shelleyan nexus", and our common admiration of De Quincey, that had chiefly brought us together; my wife's love of music was another bond between us, and many were the evenings when he came to our rooms in Gloucester Road for duets. It is of those earlier times in Shaw's career that I will now set down some personal reminiscences and anecdotes, which I think may hereafter be valued by readers who have known him only from his works.

He lived with his mother, who was a music teacher, in Fitzroy Square; and we gathered from what he used to tell us that the household was by no means in affluence. On one occasion when Mrs. Shaw had been away for a week, and had left him sufficiently provided for that time and no more, an old friend unexpectedly arrived and claimed his hospitality, with the result that he was reduced, during the remaining days, to a diet of bread and apples. Mrs. Shaw was a charming old lady, full of vivacity and wit; and it was evident that G.B.S., in spite of the levity of his talk, was very fond of her. In illustration of an argument that it is not the inevitable misfortunes, but the evitable ones, that are most distressful in life, he once wrote that his mother's death would vex him less than a misprint; and it so happened that Robert Buchanan, who was a devoted son, saw this and wrote a severe comment on it, which he sent to Shaw by post in a halfpenny wrapper. This so stirred G.B.S. that he told Buchanan that the very fact of his having sent his reproof in such a way, where it might easily have been seen by Mrs. Shaw, showed that he could not really have cared for his own mother, and that the poems which he had devoted to her memory were mere sentimentality. When G.B.S. told me this, years later, it explained a remark made to me by Robert Buchanan, which at the time rather puzzled me, that Shaw was "extremely brutal".

Shaw's mother, in her old age, took to a mild form of spiritualism, which he condoned as in her case a harmless amusement. Once, when she told him she had been in communication with the spirit of Oscar Wilde, he begged her to ask Wilde whether he remembered a certain walk they had taken together in some bygone year. A few days later the old lady said that she had delivered the message, and that Wilde remembered the occasion very well. "Then tell him he is a liar," said G.B.S., "for we never took that walk at all."

At the time when Shaw was frequently coming up to our rooms in Gloucester Road for duets with my wife he was beginning to be famous as a musical critic, and she more than once tried to enlist his aid on behalf of nascent genius; but his distrust of all such aspirants was so great as to make him blind at times even to real merit. He was urgently asked to come in one evening to hear the playing of young Donald Tovey, son of one of my former colleagues at Eton, who afterwards fully established the reputation that was already foreseen for him. The lad duly arrived, gave his performance and went; but of the critic there was no sign. After midnight there came the well-known thunderous knock; and when I opened the door the tall form on the step asked me in hoarse, anxious tones: "Has that awful boy gone?" On another occasion it was a brilliant young American, personally unknown to Shaw, who was the artist; and the invitation to give an opinion on *his* deserts brought only a postcard: "I know that American. He thinks he will set the Thames on fire. He won't."

In those days Shaw used to lunch at a vegetarian restaurant, the "Orange Grove", where I often met him. He always sat at the same table, and left a penny for the waitress. When at last she told him that she was leaving and going to be married, he said, "Come back when you're tired of him," and for the penny substituted a sovereign.

No figure was more familiar than Shaw's at the meetings of the Fabian Society, the New Fellowship, the Shelley Society, and other oganizations; and when he was not himself lecturing it was seldom that he did not join in the discussion, or put some searching question to the lecturer. One such I heard him address to a speaker at the Fabian Society — Dr. Pankhurst, I think — and then, after receiving a very lame and confused reply, he turned to me and whispered: "Did you see what sudden ruin overtook him?" He was often the Mephistopheles of the debate.

He was very sarcastic at the expense of a lecturer at a New Fellowship meeting, whose subject was "the cultivation of a perfect character"; and he told me that, years later, happening to meet the same speaker again, he was amused to hear him still harping on the same theme. As a rule, Shaw's criticisms were not unkindly in the way they were expressed; but once, when a learned Scottish professor lectured before the Fellowship, and left his audience in bewildered amazement as to his meaning, there was a rather uncomfortable scene. Asked by the chairman to speak, Shaw rose and said curtly: "Mr. Chairman, my mind is a perfect blank"; then, being unwisely pressed to state his views, he informed the unfortunate *savant* that he had been bored by him "as he had never been bored before". That he felt some remorse for this outburst was certain; and when his victim, years afterwards, sent him, as a sign of kindly feeling, a new book that he had published, Shaw, as he told me, conceived the idea of atoning for his former cruelty by writing a pleasant review. "But when I looked into the book," he added, "I felt all my old feelings return."

I think he himself repeated the story of how he shocked the Shelley Society by commencing a speech with the words: "I, as a socialist, an atheist, and a vegetarian . . ." Later, when the Shelley Centenary was calling forth some vapid apologies for the poets of free-thought, Shaw suggested that a memorial should be erected showing Shelley "in a tall hat, Bible in hand, leading his children on Sunday morning to the church of his native parish".

His opinion, at that time, of the Church of England was by no means a flattering one. I once heard him endeavour to dissuade a young friend of mine from becoming a candidate for ordination. "Are you aware," he said, "that this Church, which

163

you wish to enter, is an organized villainy?'' His advice was not accepted. Some thirty or more years later, when I was talking with the same friend, who had long been in holy orders, I ventured, with some trepidation, to ask whether he remembered what G.B.S. had said on the occasion referred to. He laughed, and answered: ''Yes, I do; and I know now that he was right.'' Shaw, at a later date, was not the atheist that he proclaimed himself to the Shelley Society; but I think his ''God'' was rather a sort of domesticated deity than what is usually understood by the term. He was once accosted by a Salvationist with the usual question, ''Are you saved?'' and his answer was an emphatic ''No!'' This, he said, took the man sharply aback; whereas a less definite reply would have left room for further molestation.

As a lecturer himself, his use of paradox kept the audience from taking anything for granted; as when, after speaking of the evils of drink, he proceeded: ''And now we come to that grave, that difficult question — how to get rid of the teetotallers.'' In a lecture which he gave in Stewart Headlam's rooms he concluded by saying that having made himself ''thoroughly misunderstood'', he would resume his seat; whereat an old gentleman rose, with a dazed expression, and asked whether Mr. Shaw had not expressed himself wrongly. So practised a speaker was he that he sometimes took liberties which might have been dangerous: he told me, for instance, that once, when lecturing, he fell into a train of thought about a Fabian lady of our acquaintance, and suddenly awoke, as it were, with a start, to find that he had not the least recollection of what he had been saying to the audience, though he judged from their unperturbed faces that he had kept the tenor of his argument.

Shaw was never more delightful than when staying with us in our cottage at Tilford, or later at Oxted; and his pretended dislike of the country added a zest to his visits. A very wet weekend at Tilford, with a Sunday walk to Gallows Hill on Hindhead, gave him a subject for a lugubrious article in the *Pall Mall Gazette* (April 28, 1888), in which he anathematized the rural life, and brought on himself a severe reproof from the editor of a Farnham paper whose strong point was not a sense of humour. My father-in-law, the Rev. J. L. Joynes, Lower Master of Eton, was also troubled by this article; and it was with some misgiving that I had the pleasure of introducing the writer to him. I afterwards remarked to Shaw that we had got through all right. "Got through!" he cried. "Why, he loves me as his own son."

On one occasion, at Oxted, I went with him to call on a Fabian family in the neighbourhood, and we found the eldest son of our friend, a boy of five or six years, busily engaged in hammering on the back of a tortoise. When we left the house, Shaw ventured on a prophecy: "Now, mark my word," he said, "that boy will be the champion criminal of the twentieth century." Truth compels me to record that the prediction has by no means been fulfilled.

On these visits to the country Shaw would be entirely natural and unaffected. He was often very tired after his labours in London; and I have seen him sit at the breakfast-table with a forlorn expression, turning perhaps the pages of the Army and Navy Co-operative Society's catalogue, and sadly shaking his head if a remark were made to him. No greater contrast to the G.B.S. on the war-path could have been imagined. We had the real pleasure of seeing that he felt at home. He wrote to me, years after: "My old visits to Oxted were quite unlike my other experience of the sort, and occupied a place of their own in my life." In my *Seventy Years Among Savages* I have spoken of the exemplary manner in which he played his part in the household duties, such as the "washing up" after meals. He had his own way of making his bed: no one else might touch it.

It was about that time, I think, that Belfort Bax bought himself a tandem tricycle, on which he used to invite a friend to accompany him on country rides; and as he was himself very lazy, and left most of the hard work to his companion, the honour was not so fully appreciated as might have been thought. We had an amusing postcard from Shaw, unfortunately not preserved, in which he narrated how he had undergone "compulsory Baxination", and how, as the pair went through a town on their steed, the bystanders could just restrain their laughter until the lanky Bax, who rode in the front, had passed them, but were visibly convulsed by the time Shaw himself came level. We suspected that G.B.S. did himself less than justice in attributing to Bax's figure the whole source of the merriment.

In view of his later prowess as a motorist, "devastating the Welsh mountains," as he wrote to me, "in a new 23-60 h.p.", I recall the fact that to drive a horse was never one of G.B.S.'s accomplishments. At a tea-party at William Morris's works at Merton Abbey, when a question arose about getting back to the railway station, someone asked Shaw if he could drive. With an infinitely sad gesture he replied: "Do I look like it?" And certainly he didn't. He once proposed that all horse-traction should be prohibited.

I several times accompanied him on day-trips to the homes of Socialist or literary acquaintances. At one, a newly furnished villa in the suburbs, the floors had just been stained by the ladies of the family with bullocks' blood. Shaw said nothing, until the question of a *name* for the house was mooted, when he suggested, with emphasis, "Goreville".

Our most notable excursion was when we went to Putney, at the invitation of Mr. Watts-Dunton, to a vegetarian lunch at "The Pines", and there met the author of *Atalanta in Calydon*. On this occasion G.B.S. was recklessly talkative as usual, Swinburne silent and constrained; and the impression left on my mind was that the poet viewed the Socialist with a feeling akin to dismay. What Shaw's thoughts were may be guessed from the fact that, in a letter written many years after, he referred to our hosts as "those two poor old blighters", and alluded to the guarded account given in my "Seventy Years" as "fearfully hypocritical". So, too, in the same letter, he would have it that his offer to go down with me to Boxhill, and there to out-talk George Meredith, was a proposal of mine; but he had the candour to admit: "Everybody thinks your account so characteristic of *me*." He added, as "the tragic sequel", that he did, at a later date, do the very thing which I had represented him as in jest offering to do; when he was forced, against his will, to talk all through the lunch, with Meredith, "distant and deaf", trying to catch what he was saying.

Shaw was indeed a great talker; his stories were inexhaustible, and did not quite fall under De Quincey's verdict that "all anecdotes are false", for there was usually just a kernel of truth in them, however much the subject might be enlarged and embellished. His family history furnished material for a number of these tales, among which perhaps that of his uncle's suicide, by throwing himself into a portmanteau, was the most picturesque. He once told this in print, in the weekly column of musical criticism which he contributed to the *Star* under the name of

"Corno di Bassetto"; and when I addressed some verses to him on the subject, these appeared the following week, with the remark that the man who can make a jest of a family affliction must be dead to feeling.

His own love-affairs figured largely in anecdote. I will mention only one of them, his earliest, in Dublin, which, as we learnt from him, was broken off in anger by the lady because when they were out walking together he was so tired that he "could not go a step further", and was compelled to tell her so. Nor were other persons' love-affairs forgotten; and when we inquired how it was that they were so rash as to entrust a secret to him, he assured us that they all selected him as being the safest of confidants. He was struck by the coincidence that two married ladies, to each of whom he had ventured to put the question *why* she had married her husband, replied in the same words: "Because I had never known anyone else."

Complaints were sometimes heard of his lack of politeness. He explained publicly that as a young man he used to be polite, and would even jump up to open doors for ladies, and so on; until one day a female relative said to him: "George, don't be officious: women don't like it." He had never been polite since then.

When we first knew him he was practically unknown as a writer; and I remember his announcing that his reputation was "going up by leaps and bounds", because one of his novels, *Cashel Byron* perhaps, had sold to the tune of about a dozen copies in the year instead of half that number. This improvement was maintained, until he felt able to tell his friend H. W. Massingham, editor of the *Daily Chronicle*, that he would no longer accept broken sums, pounds, shillings and pence, for his contributions to that journal, but in future would expect five pounds for anything that he wrote. Mr. Massingham told him that by this rash demand he had done for himself as far as the *Chronicle* was concerned; and weeks passed without any further communications. Then Shaw got a letter from "H.W.M." asking for an article on some specified subject, and adding: "Have your own damned terms." But even at a later period Shaw felt no entire confidence in his future. Mr. W. Robinson, owner of *The Garden* and other papers, asked me to approach him on his behalf, with a proposal that he should edit a new food-reform journal then in contemplation, to be entitled *Grub*. Shaw shrugged his shoulders, and merely remarked: ''I may come even to that.'' But as Fortune smiled on him he became more assured. A firm of solicitors once offered to finance him in a slander action against the Prince of Wales (afterwards King Edward VII), on account of a remark made by H.R.H. to the manager of a theatre about one of his plays, that the author ''must be mad''. Shaw's magnanimous answer was that as he would not prosecute an ordinary man in such a case, he must not make any exception when dealing with royalty.

His affectation of a sense of greatness, long before the general public was aware of him, was most entertaining. I heard a lady say to him: ''Shaw, when you are famous ———.'' He interrupted, with pretended amazement: ''*When* I am famous!'' Asked if he ever read any books, he replied emphatically, ''None''; but immediately continued: ''Except my own; which I read with ever-increasing admiration.'' But he was not always thus flattered in private circles. I remember, when he had just written *Candida*, how he read it to a few friends in our rooms, and at the end, as we were giving our various opinions, Edward Carpenter said curtly: ''No, Shaw. It won't do.'' On another occasion he recited to me, as we were walking along Oxford Street, some verses that he had written in celebration, it seemed, of a suicide who had thrown himself down from a height. The only lines which I afterwards could recall ran thus: ''And when he bashed his bloody head Upon the bloody ground.'' Those two were fixed in my memory, because, as he shouted them aloud to make them audible above the din of the traffic, I noticed the startled face of a passer-by.

Together with Professor Graham Wallas I was a witness of Bernard Shaw's marriage to Miss Payne Townshend at the Henrietta Street Register Office in June 1898. He was then recovering from an operation on his foot, and had acquired much dexterity in hopping on one leg, in which manner he entered the Registrar's presence, rather to the surprise, as it seemed, of that grave official. The humorous account of the ceremony, published in the *Star* of June 2, was written by Shaw himself. Who else would have described the marriage as ''the second operation'' which Mr. Shaw had lately undergone, and one against which Mr. Salt, as hon. secretary of the Humanitarian League, ''would naturally have remonstrated had there been time''?

Unfortunately there was in fact another surgical operation in store for Shaw a few weeks after his marriage; and, as he wrote to me, "in order to make my recovery a thorough test for vegetarianism", he also fell downstairs and broke an arm. He *did* recover; and few things written by him are more diverting than his message printed in the *Academy* (October 15, 1898), with an illustration of himself as "The Dying Vegetarian", and directions for his funeral, which was to be followed by a representative procession of the animals whom he had not eaten.

When I was staying with the Shaws in the house on Hindhead where these tragedies took place, a neighbour, a country gentleman, happened to call, and when asked what he had been doing lately, said, "Oh, I have been shooting." The look on his face indicated nothing less than bewilderment when Shaw, in a tone of kindly surprise, inquired: "Why on earth did you do that?" It will be remembered that Shaw's description of his own recreations in *Who's Who* were "anything except sport".

In a letter of 1903 Shaw wrote: "Have you read Samuel Butler's posthumous *Way of All Flesh*? It is one of the great books of the world. You will throw Shelley, Thomson, Meredith, and all the rest out of the window, and take Butler to your heart for ever." I had been struck, when lunching at Adelphi Terrace in Samuel Butler's presence, by the almost filial respect with which he was treated, the only instance in which I ever saw Shaw show any feeling of the kind. He had lost his faith in "great men" at an early age: he said that in the case of William Rossetti he was sorry to abandon it; in Butler's it seemed unexpectedly to have returned.

The brilliance of Shaw's "table-talk" was a constant joy to his friends; I have often thought that in this respect his true forerunner was Sydney Smith. Was he ever "scored off" in his encounter with other wits? The only case I heard of was when he asked an oculist whether there was anything unusual about his eyes, and received the reply: "Oh no! You're one of those damned normals. There are only ten per cent of them."

There is no fear that insufficient justice will be done to Shaw's humour. What is likely to be overlooked is something closely allied to his humour — his humanity. A hater of sport and vivisection, he was also a consistent vegetarian. When told how an acquaintance had been saying that he, too, would abjure meat, were it not for the sake of his dear wife and children, Shaw's only comment was: "Scoundrel!" He also disliked vegetarians of the flowery and sentimental sort; for instance, Anna Kingsford. He told me once, when she was lecturing, he laid a trap for her in a question of a hard, practical kind, which she might think came from one of the unconverted. She rose, with great dignity, and answered, "Sir; I am a vegetarian"; to which Shaw made the prompt rejoinder: "And so am I."

He was a great lover of cats; and when he came to see us never failed to ask after "Cosy". Were there more kittens? Then he would add in a contemplative tone: "She is a cat of fearful passions." At his rooms in Fitzroy Square there used often to be a neighbouring cat, or a stray, in his company. Once one who was sitting on his window-sill, on the first floor, jumped or fell into the area below. He said he rushed in horror to look out, but no cat was visible, and he feared the concussion had been so great that the animal had disappeared in fine dust.

His objection to vaccination was often expressed. He had smallpox himself when he first came to town; and feeling ill, but not knowing what was the matter, decided that to spend a day or two in riding round London on the top of an omnibus would perhaps be of benefit. This he did (and afterwards speculated on the number of persons he had infected); then, feeling no better, went to a doctor and discovered the truth.

It was dangerous, as many reformers found to their cost, to ask Shaw to bless their own cause, or to curse the opposing one: he was apt to say the thing that was not expected of him. But on one subject he never wavered or changed — where some humanitarian interest was at stake. My final impression of him might be summed up in some verses printed in *The Times* on the occasion of his seventieth birthday, in which the question was asked for which of his qualities — his fun, his seriousness, his illuming thought, his dramatic genius — the future would praise him; and the conclusion was as follows:

> All these: but most, that wit so keen
> Could flash from heart so kind.

March, 1929

[This essay made its first appearance in Winsten's *Salt and His Circle*. For Shaw's "corrections", see Winsten's book, pages 205–217. Eds]

# IV
# SALT AS
# CORRESPONDENT

A quiet, unassuming, yet witty man who enjoyed good company, Salt had a wide circle of friends and acquaintances in socialist, rationalist, humanitarian, literary, and publishing circles, and he kept in touch with them in person or by mail. We have chosen a few of his letters for inclusion in this anthology, and in the Mahatma Gandhi section we include both sides of the correspondence.

EDITORS

## M. K. GANDHI

Early in his student days (1888 – 1891) in London, M. K. Gandhi was dissatisfied with the food available to him. He finally found a vegetarian restaurant, and as he entered it he saw a copy of Salt's *A Plea for Vegetarianism* and purchased it. He was convinced by Salt's logic and wrote many years later in his *Autobiography*: "From the date of reading this book, I may claim to have become a vegetarian by choice." Salt and Gandhi apparently met in May of 1891 when both spoke at the Conference of the Vegetarian Federal Union, and they met at least one other time in Salt's office.

On September 18, 1929, Salt wrote Gandhi, then engaged in the struggle to win Indian independence:

> You will hardly remember me; but I had the honour of seeing mention of my book, "A Plea for Vegetarianism," in a translation of your Autobiography, and I once saw you, I think, at the office of the Humanitarian League in London. On the strength of this, I am taking the liberty of writing to you.
>
> Some forty years ago I published a Life of Thoreau, the author of that remarkable book, "Walden"; and an American friend of mine is now collecting material for a new and fuller Life, for which purpose I am handing over to him the various letters and press-notices that are in my possession. In the last letter which I received from this friend, Mr. Raymond Adams, of North Carolina, he asked me whether I thought that *you* had been a reader of Thoreau, and had been at all influenced by him, as on many subjects your views and Thoreau's seem rather akin. Not being able to answer his question, I told him I would venture to write to you direct and ask you. That is the cause of this letter.[1]

[[1]Though his study of Thoreau engaged his attention for many years, Professor Adams never published the Thoreau biography.   Eds.]

I have been a vegetarian close on fifty years, and it has greatly benefited me, both in health, and in what is still more important, in spirit. I was much interested by what you wrote on the subject in your Autobiography. . . .

## Gandhi answered Salt's letter on October 12, 1929:

I was agreeably surprised to receive your letter. Yes, indeed your book which was the first English book I came across on vegetarianism was of immense help to me in steadying my faith in vegetarianism. My first introduction to Thoreau's writings was, I think, in 1907, or late [r], when I was in the thick of [the] passive resistance struggle. A friend sent me Thoreau's essay on civil disobedience. It left a deep impression upon me. I translated a portion of that essay for the readers of Indian Opinion in South Africa which I was then editing, and I made copious extracts from that essay for that paper. That essay seemed to be so convincing and truthful that I felt the need of knowing more of Thoreau, and I came across your Life of him, his "Walden" and other short essays, all of which I read with great pleasure and equal profit.

## Salt responded to Gandhi on December 2, 1929:

May I thank you for your letter of October 12th, which was of great interest both to myself and to my American friend who is writing a Life of Thoreau.

As to Vegetarianism, I feel much honoured by your saying that my book on that subject was of help to you.

As you doubtless have read, all good causes have suffered a loss this year by the death of Edward Carpenter. I had known him well for some forty five years, and miss him very much. But death came as a release to him, for he had been very ill for over a year.

After beginning this correspondence with Gandhi, Salt wrote this poem:

INDIA IN 1930

An India governed, under alien law
    By royal proclamation,
By force, by pomp of arms, that fain would awe
    Her newly-wakened nation;
While he who sways the heart of Hindustan,
    To more than Kingship risen,
Is one old, powerless, unresisting man,
    Whose palace is—a prison.

*Cum Grano*

When Gandhi was in England in 1931, he gave a speech on November 20 at a meeting of the London Vegetarian Society. Salt was present and was honoured in Gandhi's opening remarks: "When I received the invitation to be present at this meeting," Gandhi began, "I need not tell you how pleased I was, because it revived old memories and recollections of pleasant friendships formed with vegetarians. I feel especially honoured [to have] on my right Mr. Henry Salt. It was Mr. Salt's book, *A Plea for Vegetarianism*, which showed me why, apart from a hereditary habit, and apart from my adherence to a vow administered to me by my mother, it was right to be a vegetarian. He showed me why it was a moral duty incumbent on vegetarians not to live upon fellow-animals. It is, therefore, a matter of additional pleasure to me that I find Mr. Salt in our midst." Gandhi concluded his speech with another mention of Salt, who had been a member of the Society for over forty years.

Almost a year after receiving those words of praise from one of the most famous men of the twentieth century, Salt wrote Gandhi on October 8, 1932:

> Since I had the honour of meeting you in November last I have often thought of writing to you; and being now an octogenarian, and my life drawing near its close, I will no longer delay. I have the more reason to write because I wish to express to you the sympathy and admiration with which I have read of your recent efforts for the welfare of India.
>
> The subject under special consideration, when I saw you in London, was Vegetarianism; and I feel as strongly as ever that food-reform, like Socialism, has an essential part to play in the liberation of man-kind. I cannot see how there be any real and full recognition of Kinship, as long as men continue either to *cheat*, or to *eat*, their fellow-beings!

Gandhi wrote these notes at the top of the letter: "I thank you for your letter. May I say in all humility that one rarely finds people outside India recognizing nonhuman beings as fellow-beings. Millenium [*sic*] will have come when mankind generally recognises and acts up to this grand truth. Thank you."

Text adapted from Hendrick's *Henry Salt*.
The Gandhi-Salt correspondence appeared in
*Company I Have Kept* and Hendrick's *Henry Salt*.

## *RICHARD BENTLEY*

Salt had been interested in Thoreau for many years and on November 28, 1889, he submitted his manuscript on the poet-naturalist to Richard Bentley, the London publisher:

> I send herewith the *MS* of my Life of Thoreau.
>
> I have still to add to it some more papers promised me from America. Also I hope to get the letters addressed by Thoreau to the only Englishman who became well acquainted with him — a Mr. Cholmondeley, nephew to Bishop Heber. Otherwise, with the exception of a short appendix of bibliography, &c, the work is complete.
>
> Of the letters I have inserted so far, the majority are cited from the volume published at Boston in 1865, and a few are unprinted ones.

Salt had never been to the United States and at that time did not have good informants, as he later had, to help him gather information about Thoreau. Even in England, he found little interest from anyone to assist him with his research: the Cholmondeley letters were not located for him, though they were finally found and turned over to F. B. Sanborn.

Salt was apparently not offered the best of terms for his manuscript. He wrote Bentley on January 6, 1890:

> I am glad to hear that you like my Thoreau manuscript and are favourably inclined towards its publication.
>
> As to the terms, would you be willing to let the royalty commence

after the sale of 500, instead of 750, copies? By that time the book would, I presume, have paid its way, and if the edition consists of 1000 copies there would still be a chance for the author of receiving some remuneration on this edition, which would scarcely be the case if 750 copies had first to be disposed of. I do not know what your intentions are as to the number of copies to be printed, but I am assuming that it would be 1000.

I suppose, in the event of your publishing the book, you would be able to bring it out in the spring of the year?

Salt's 1890 biography of Thoreau did not sell well, and he wrote Bentley on October 10, 1895, at a time when a new and expanded version was in progress: "I am sorry, for your sake as well as my own, that the book fared so badly."

> Letters in Rare Book Room and Special Collections,
> University of Illinois at Urbana-Champaign Library.
> Published by John T. Flanagan in *NEQ* 28 (June, 1955).

## W. S. KENNEDY

Salt first met W. S. Kennedy, Whitman's friend, at the home of Edward Carpenter, but Salt had even earlier corresponded with Kennedy. He wrote to Kennedy on August 30, 1889:

> My friend Edward Carpenter, whom I believe you know, tells me that he thinks you might possibly be able to give me some help towards a biography of Thoreau — I am working at a volume in which I wish to combine a clear and comprehensive account of Thoreau's life with a fuller and more serious estimate of his doctrines than those given in the existing memoirs — Mr. Harrison Blake has kindly promised to give me what assistance he can, and so have some other friends and students of Thoreau.
>
> If you should chance to know of any out-lying sources of information, or unpublished letters, I should be very much obliged to you if you would tell me of them. . . .

The correspondence between 1889 and 1920 is missing; it resumes here with Salt's letter dated February 15, 1921, after *Seventy Years Among Savages* had appeared:

I will not delay to send a line to thank you, and Mrs. Kennedy, for your kind letters about those Savages. I value your opinion; especially what you say about the chapter on Death and Love. Will you tell Mrs. Kennedy that Eton boys *are* (as she was informed) very well-bred, and if they pour slops on the heads of passers-by in the street, they do it in the handsomest manner. The book has had an extraordinarily "good press" in this country, commencing with *The Times* (enclosed) on the day of publication, and all the other papers, or some fifty of them, including *Punch*, following on similar lines. I am the "Faddist", of course; but they take kindly to the role of savages. A few reviews have been reasoned and serious; most of them evade the moral, and go for the anecdotes.

So you saw and heard "G.K.C."! [G. K. Chesterton] He is a very clever fellow, so whimsical in his wit; not a clear thinker, or a trustworthy guide, but unsurpassed in certain forms of humour. I am sorry he was out of England just at the time my book appeared, as I think it might have drawn something good from him.

You mention Herman Melville. It is strange that no biography of him has appeared. *Twice* have I had letters from countrymen of yours (the first was Arthur Stedman, son of the well-known writer, I forget who the second was [John Freeman]), announcing that they were engaged on such a work; but neither one nor the other stuck to it. I sent over all the material I had, for the use of one of them, and never got it back. Mrs. Melville was then living in New York, I believe, with a daughter; but now I have not heard of them for many years and don't know if they are still alive.

No, I think the "Whale" is his chief work, in spite of its many faults, transcendentalism, &c. I introduced it to William Morris's notice, and he truly enjoyed it. So did Robert Buchanan, & others; but somehow Melville does not "catch on", even in "Typee" which is of course the most artistic of his books. I wrote an Introduction years ago for John Murrey's Ed. of "Typee" and "Omoo". . . . I hope you will get out your Whitman handbook. . . .

Salt did not find Raymond Weaver's biography of Melville an impressive piece of work, but his admiration for *Moby-Dick* was undiminished. He wrote Kennedy on April 23, 1923:

Yours of April 1st to hand. I was glad to see what you say of "Moby Dick"; it is a marvellous book. There seems to be a revival of interest here in Melville, at least among the better informed. I could wish that Weaver had woven his materials more skilfully in the *Life*; the book seems to me at fault, in its attempts at Epigram and cleverness on the biographer's part, while there is no real or vivid presentment of Melville himself.

Like you, I have to *skip* freely in reading "Moby Dick". Melville suffered severely from the epidemic of Transcendentalism. But when one knows where to read, and where to skip, all is well. . . .

Salt remarried after the death of his first wife. He wrote Kennedy on March 30, 1927:

. . . On Friday last I married Catherine Mandeville, my housekeeper, and have thus feathered my nest for old age, by securing a most affectionate and devoted companionship.

Seventy-five married to thirty-five sounds strange; but when you see you'll understand how wise I've been and congratulate me. The loneliness of the last decade has been intolerable.

Salt, a Classics scholar, published a verse translation of Virgil's *AEneid*, which was praised by Kennedy. Salt wrote Kennedy on December 25, 1928:

I need not tell you that I am much gratified to learn, from your letter of Dec. 12th, that you think so well of my Virgil translation. Virgil has meant a great deal to me; and now that the book is actually published, which I scarcely dared to hope ever to see, it is of course a great pleasure to me to find that it gives satisfaction to other lovers of the poet, like yourself, who appreciate him too well to be put off with any inferior stuff.

There have not, as yet, been a great number of press-notices—, not more than half-a-dozen of any real importance—, but so far they have been on the whole very favourable, especially about the choice of metre, which they grossly acclaim as "the true formula". In several cases, too, they express the opinion that this is the best of the published versions.

I could hardly expect more than this, without being as unreasonable as some poets are! And I don't consider myself a *poet*; so that I by no means resent such (just) criticisms as that my verse is "always poetical, never poetry". I hope that some real poet, instead of adopting a *wrong* medium, as Dryden did, will some day use the right one, and produce a translation that is itself a poem. For I look on the Englishing of Virgil as, so to speak, a social task, not a merely individual one; in the sense that any one who attempts it should be glad if his successors can make use of his efforts and build something better thereon. That is how I feel, any how, about my own version. . . .

None of the critics have quoted from Book VI, in which I think I have succeeded best, and which (in my opinion) Virgil surpasses even himself. Well, I keep your letter among my treasures.

Catherine and I are getting through the winter somehow; and when this swinish festival of Christmas is over, I shall feel more hope for the new year. . . .

Letters at Rollins College.
Published by George Hendrick in
*ESQ* 19 (II Quarter, 1960).

## DR. SAMUEL ARTHUR JONES

One of Salt's most interesting correspondents was Dr. Samuel Arthur Jones, homoeopathic physician in Ann Arbor, Michigan, and amateur Thoreau scholar. It was Dr. Jones, a fiery Welshman, who provided Salt much valuable information for the 1896 revised edition of the Thoreau biography. For more details about the literary friendship of Salt and Dr. Jones and for a more comprehensive selection of Salt's letters to Dr. Jones see Fritz Oehlschlaeger and George Hendrick, *Toward the Making of Thoreau's Modern Reputation* (University of Illinois Press, 1979).

Salt wrote to Dr. Jones on June 30, 1890:

I have to thank you for your two letters, full of kind thoughts and friendly encouragement which I assure you I value very highly.

And first, about Thoreau. It is very kind of you to send me the proof of your new bibliography, which I shall read with much interest. But I am sorry to say it will be too late to enable me to make additions to mine, as the *Life* is already printed off, "with all its imperfections on its head" — like Hamlet's father! It strikes me, however, that I may still be able to help *you*, if I chance to have hit upon any mention of Thoreau which may not have caught your attention; I therefore enclose one of the rough proofs of my own bibliography, or rather of that part of it in which there is likely to be any divergence. There are a good many things in it which are not included in your earlier bibliography, but I daresay you have filled up many of them ere now. Of course both your compilation and mine will very soon be out-of-date, as there will doubtless be a crop of Thoreau articles when these books make their appearance.

My book will be published by Bentley in the autumn. I am also editing (I forget whether I told you this) a volume of selected Essays from the "Anti-Slavery & Reform Papers" for Messrs. Sonnenschein's *Social Science Series* of half-crown volumes. The Essays included are "Civil Disobedience", "Plea for John Brown", "Last Days of John Brown", "Paradise (to be) Regained", and "Life without Principle" — I should have liked to include *all* the essays, but this could not be managed; I hope, however, the volume may serve to create more interest in Thoreau; and as it will be issued at the same time as the *Life*, the two books will help one another. Messrs. Sonnenschein think of following it up with another volume of "Excursions", if it is fairly successful. I may add that my introductory note, or part of it, to the "Anti-Slavery" reprint, is to appear in magazine form in the August number of *Lippincott* (English Edition).[1]

So you see there is to be quite a carnival of Thoreauism this autumn, which will be swelled still further by Mr. Blake's volume of selections, and possibly by yet another which an Edinburgh publisher has in preparation! It should be a worthy answer to the malignant criticism of Lowell and his followers.

As to the *Letters*, you will, I am sure, understand my position. Mr. Sanborn [a Thoreau scholar disliked by Dr. Jones] has been exceedingly courteous and kind to me in helping me with the *Life*, and I would not on any account do anything which could be construed into a slight on him. He has, I rather think, possession of the bulk of these letters, and may (justly, perhaps) consider himself the best person to edit them. *Prima facie* it would certainly appear desirable that they should be edited by someone on the *spot*; and I should be well content to help by trying to secure the letters, which I really believe are still extant in England, addressed by Thoreau to his English friend Thomas Cholmondeley. I had quite hoped to get them for my own book, but, owing to the illness and apparent dilatoriness of Mr. C's surviving brother, I was so far disappointed. On the whole, probably Mr. Blake [Thoreau's literary executor] will do wisely to wait and see my "Life of Thoreau" before coming to any decision; but you may feel sure that I shall be glad to help in any part, great or small, which is likely to be of service to Thoreau's memory.

I may here remark that I do not of course regard my "Life of Thoreau" as in any sense a full or *final* biography. I only aim at doing what really ought to have been done twenty years ago, viz — giving a clear and succinct account of the man and his writings, and gathering together all the fragmentary records of him. I hope it may form a stepping-stone to a final *Life*, which must be written on the spot, and by someone who has full use of all the manuscript diaries and letters.

And now I must thank you still further for your kindness in sending me the photographs in the charge of Dr. Carrow. It will be a great pleasure to me to see Dr. Carrow, and have some talk about Thoreau, and American friends, and I need not tell how much interested I shall be in the photographs. The reproduction of the earlier portrait has been done very nicely by Messrs. Bentley's artist, and will, I think, form a good frontispiece to my volume; but of course it would have been more satisfactory if we could have had *two* portraits of Thoreau, one before he wore the beard, and one after. This however was more than the publishers were prepared to do, as they are not at all certain of the pecuniary success of the volume. I confess I do not much care for the portrait prefixed to Mr. Sanborn's book;[2] the beard seems to hide the distinctive traits of Thoreau's features. But I must not express an opinion until I have seen your photograph, which is perhaps a different one.

Your kind suggestion about a possible opening for me at Harvard University makes me feel certain that I should at any rate find one good friend in America, were I to cross the Atlantic! But for various reasons it would be impossible for me to think of leaving this country — one alone would be imperative, that my wife and I have both relatives whom we could not leave at present. Otherwise I am not specially bound to England *as* England, and I have much faith in the greatness and greatheartedness of the American people, in spite of the truth of Thoreau's strictures. However I hope that you and I may manage to meet some day. Do you ever come on a visit to England?

I am glad to hear you feel an interest in Edward Carpenter's writings, and I will ask Messrs. Sonnenschein, his publishers, to forward his two volumes of essays to the address you name, in the most convenient way. Please accept them from me; and if you would afterwards like to see his "Towards Democracy", a strange, original sort of poem, in Whitmanese metre, that could follow later. He is a most remarkable personality, with much of the Thoreau element in him, and much too of Whitman. He was formerly curate to the great broad-churchman, Frederick Denison Maurice, at Cambridge; but under the stress of new convictions, gave up his College Fellowship, left the Church, and is now a Socialist and advocate of various reforms, especially of a simplification of life which is very like that of Thoreau.

It seems to me that the hope of society lies in finding the balance between the just claims of socialism, which certainly will be heard more and more loudly each year, and the equally just claims of an intellectual (not commercial) individualism, such as that which Thoreau preached so finely. The true individualism, as I understand it, consists not in the freedom to cheat one's neighbour, but in the freedom to develop one's own intellect. At present our so-called "freedom" is mostly of the former kind.

I was particularly glad to hear that my little book on Shelley had been of interest to you. Believe me that when Shelley is rightly understood (as he cannot be under our existing system of morality which is really *im*morality), he will be recognised as one of the truly great characters of this century — the poet without an equal since Shakespeare, and one of the most clear-sighted prophets of social reform. Unlike as he is to Thoreau in many ways, they are alike in this, that both were champions of the great humanitarian movement which will be *the* religion of the future, and both have that unspeakable tenderness which is for ever misunderstood by the mere critic, but endears them beyond all expression to those who are in sympathy.

[P.S.] You will see that I have put Theodore Watts's name to two *Athenaeum* articles in 1877 and 1882 respectively.[3] I have his authority for this. He professes to be a great admirer of Thoreau, from the point of view of a lover of Nature, and he tells me he introduced Thoreau's works to George Borrow, who greatly relished them.

You mention Dr. Japp. I have corresponded with him at times, but have never met him personally, some obstacle having always unfortunately intervened when we had hoped to meet. I like the *tone* of his book on Thoreau, though the book itself is scarcely satisfactory. I have met Mr. Dircks, and know his Prefaces on

Thoreau, but must confess I don't admire them — at the risk of appearing like a workman who abuses his predecessors! The Essays I do greatly admire are those by John Weiss, in the *Christian Examiner*, and by John Burroughs in the *Century*; also Higginson's chapter, in his *Short Studies*.

1. Salt's essay "Anti-Slavery and Reform Papers" appeared in the English edition of *Lippincott's Magazine*, August 1890, pp. 277–83.

2. Sanborn used the ambrotype of Thoreau made in 1861 by E. S. Dunshee in New Bedford.

3. [Theodore Watts], "Review of Page's *Thoreau, His Life and Aims*," *Athenaeum*, November 3, 1877, 562–64. "Review of Early Spring in Massachusetts and Sanborn's Life of Thoreau," *Athenaeum* 2 (October 28, 1882):558–60.

Dr. Jones's man-on-the-Concord-scene was Fred Hosmer, who made many important Thoreau finds which were shared with Salt. Hosmer was also a gifted photographer, and his Concord scenes are now to be found in the Concord Public Library and the University of Illinois Library. Salt wrote Dr. Jones on July 16, 1893, about Hosmer photographs and about F. B. Sanborn, who had known Thoreau, Emerson, and Alcott:

A few weeks ago I received a delightful present of Thoreau photographs from Mr. Hosmer, of Concord, and this set me again attempting to induce some English publisher to issue an illustrated volume of Thoreau — whether *Walden* or one of the other works. But I have met with no success whatever up to the present; for publishers one & all seem afraid to venture on Thoreau, and I daresay they are right enough in a *commercial* view of the matter!

Mr. Sanborn has been in London lately, but only on a flying visit, as he was returning to America from the east of Europe, where he has been spending the winter and spring. I went up to London one afternoon and had an hour's talk with him. I had received, a week or so before I saw him, his new *Life of Alcott*, which doubtless you have read or looked through before now. I was rather disappointed at not finding more about Thoreau in the book, though one or two of the references are interesting. Sanborn talks of publishing another volume of Thoreau letters shortly. . . .[1]

1. Sanborn's *Familiar Letters of Henry David Thoreau* was published in 1894.

Rare Book and Special Collections, University of Illinois at Urbana-Champaign Library. First published in *Toward the Making of Thoreau's Modern Reputation*

## JOSEPH ISHILL

The American publisher Joseph Ishill first came across *Animals' Rights*, and impressed by the form and psychology of that book sought out Salt's studies of Shelley, Thoreau, Jefferies, De Quincey, "and others which shed so pure a light on the character and significance of their lives and works." Ishill's Oriole Press published Salt's *Cum Grano* and *A Group of Unpublished Letters by Henry S. Salt to Joseph Ishill* (1942).

Ishill wrote Salt on June 23, 1930, wanting to publish a work of Salt's. Salt responded on July 12, 1930:

> I have to thank you for your very kind letter of June 23rd, with its offer to print and publish some work of mine under the auspices of the Oriole Press, a compliment which I much appreciate.
>
> You and I are akin, I know, in this way — that neither of us has had any thought of the book-market and its preferences, or has allowed considerations of that sort to determine what we should write or publish. As an instance, I may mention that I have lately been an object of suspicion to the income-tax office, because I had little income, or none, from my books, to "declare" in making my annual "return"; and it was with some difficulty that I made the office see that there are some writers who do not write for money!
>
> Well, I have been thinking over the several subjects I might offer you, and chiefly about the selection of "Poems of Love and Death" of which I spoke. I have been carefully re-reading them and considering their best arrangement; and certainly they are very beautiful and touching. Nevertheless I have a feeling that there is a *sameness* about them — the theme being always a sad one —

which might make such a collection depressing to a reader; and for that reason I am inclined to think that it might be better to take up a cheerful subject in which there would be more variety, and the opportunity of suggesting some wise and humane reflections.

In brief, I now have in mind the hitherto unpublished volume of short Epigrams of which I spoke, under title of "Cum Grano" (*salis* omitted!). I could make of it whatever length were deemed convenient; if quite short, most of the verses would be new; if moderately long, some could be re-printed from prevous pamphlets; anyhow there would be material for a volume of no great bulk.

So will you now turn this over in your mind, and then, if you approve, I shall go ahead with the scheme; or of course, if by any chance you should prefer the "Poems of Love and Death," I could still deal with them. Just to show you the sort of thing I have in view, I enclose two or three specimens, which need not be returned.

The two men decided that *Cum Grano* would be a better choice for the Oriole Press, and Salt wrote Ishill on October 21, 1930:

I am at last sending you the manuscript of my little volume of Epigrams, under the title of "Cum Grano." (I hope there *is* a grain of salt in it!)

In doing so, I want to say that you must be entirely free to print it, or *not* to print it, as you may feel disposed when you have seen the contents. I should be trespassing on your kindness if I let you think that I am one of those authors who are at all in favour with any considerable section of the public. I am not; and none of my books have ever had what a publisher would call a success. There would be no chance of *this* work repaying the cost of production. . . .

As Salt predicted, *Cum Grano* was not a financial success, but it did have a few good notices, including this one in *The Manchester City News*:

Mr. Salt has aptly named his collected epigrams "Cum Grano," leaving us to Latinise his name and finish the tag. He is our English Martial. Many years ago, as he frankly admits, he won a medal for Greek epigram at Cambridge, and he has been adroitly using the sharp weapon of verse ever since to cut into unreason and inhumanity; as he says, the light-arm versifier can do "timely service by turning a rhyme and overturning a fool." His lines are crisp; his cleverness is displayed in retort; he converts a platitudinous fallacy into an argument against the man who employs it; and he always has a high purpose in his witty encounters. Mr. Salt is, of course, a "faddist" — that is, he combats current follies, he seeks the reform of abuses, he tries to remedy evils, he puts truth in a new light, he preaches charity and good-will, he conducts a crusade on behalf of the helpless and oppressed, he puts reason in place of blindness. All very obnoxious, as pioneer work always is. Yet Mr. Salt's fiercest opponents must often be constrained to admire his smartness and to laugh at his humour. If his grains are bitter they have a refreshing savour; and if he does sometimes make a wry face they are calculated to cure a disease. In short here is an epigrammatist with fine ideals that cannot be mistaken. . . .

*A Group of Unpublished Letters by Henry S. Salt to Joseph Ishill*

## *AGNES DAVIES*

Even in advanced age, Salt made new friends, including John and Agnes Davies, who were ardent Vegetarians. Salt wrote Mrs. Davies on April 20, 1934:

Many thanks for your letter, and for the kind things there said. I have great reason to be thankful for my own good fortune in life; but I cannot help wondering whether as the years go on — thousands, and perhaps millions of them — man will be content to be the slave of fortune as now, pretending it is what is called "God's will", and will not rather become master of his own destiny, in regard to such matters at least as the date and manner of his death. That is what I had in thought when I spoke of "overstaying my time".

I was interested to hear of what you first look for in the "Vegetarian News"! Frank Wyatt, the Editor, is a most faithful champion of the cause; but I fear he overtasks himself — "burns the candle at both ends" — and his Notes in the *V.N.* suffer in consequence sometimes. I am more and more sure that it is greatly to the intellectual disadvantage of anyone to be compelled, for whatever reason, to dwell almost solely on the particular cause (vegetarianism, socialism, pacifism, or whatever it may be) and so forget the like importance of the rest. Yet there is the present difficulty; for if one does *not* centre on a special subject, nothing gets done! . . .

Salt wrote Mrs. Davies on January 27, 1935, about *The Creed of Kinship*:

It is all rather queer about the book. Constable's hurried it into type, with the intention (I guess) of showing it to Shaw complete, and so having a better chance of getting a preface from him. But he has been very ill, and is needing a change, and evidently *not* acceded to his publisher's suggestion: & the book makes a nice little vol. of 118 pages, without anything more than what is supplied by myself.

Constable's are most reticent; but I suspect that they counted too confidently on the great man, and then had gone too far with the book to drop it. All I hear from them is that perhaps Mr. Shaw will help by writing about it elsewhere (most unlikely, I should think). I ask them no questions, and don't know even the price, or the date of publication. . . .

Shaw has not been here: but in reply to a letter, nothing about the book, in which I spoke of his serious "cold", he wrote me the one enclosed, which I send more for the frivolous John's entertainment than for yours. I am inclined to think that, Shaw's view of Kinship being what it is, I am better off without a preface from him. If he had written, no one would have read a word of mine; as it is, I may get attention from a handful of people, and Constable's can bear the loss from the book! . . .

Only two years before his death, the Royal Society for the Prevention of Cruelty to Animals threatened legal action against Salt, who wrote the details to Mrs. Davies on February 16, 1937:

. . . I forget whether I told you that a member of the R.S.P.C.A. council had written to me (the second time in three years) that the

Chief Secretary was trying, privately, to win support for the legalisation of *the Lash* in bad cases of cruelty to animals. He wrote "in confidence", but I replied that I would not tolerate confidences on *that* subject, and should let friends know; which I have done. On Saturday (when I was taking a rest in bed!) my informant arrived personally in great perturbation, with the news that the Chief Secretary asserts that my letter (to him) is libellous, and threatens to bring an action. I, under legal advice, have pointed out to him that what I wrote of the horrors of flogging was in no sense personal, but an old-standing humanitarian protest; and it now remains to see if he will proceed.

I hardly think he will; because to press such a case, and to prosecute one of the oldest workers for animals, would hardly redound to the credit of the Royal Society; but I mean to be full prepared. If there *is* such a case, I shall conduct my own defence personally, and give the Court some information. Meantime it is better to be silent.

So, you see, the new house is somewhat forgotten at the moment! If we move, it will probably be in April or May. . . .

And it is possible that *I* may be in *prison* by then, if a Flogging Judge is called on to decide my libel-suit, for I certainly will not retract or apologise.

The R.S.P.C.A. apparently reconsidered and did not bring suit against Salt. In February of 1937, Salt must have felt he had lived almost ninety years among savages.

# V
# SALT'S SUMMING UP:
# THE CREED OF KINSHIP

## THE CREED OF KINSHIP

It may be well here to sum up, in the fewest possible words, the conclusions reached in this book [The *Creed of Kinship*]:

(1) That our present so called "Civilisation" is only a "manner of speaking," and is in fact quite a rude state as compared with what may already be foreseen.

(2) That the basis of any real morality must be the sense of Kinship between all living things.

(3) That there can be no abiding national welfare until the extremes of Wealth and Poverty are abolished.

(4) That Warfare will not be discontinued until we have ceased to honour soldiering as heroic.

(5) That the Rights of Animals have henceforth to be considered; and that such practices as cruel sports, vivisection, and flesh eating are not compatible with civilised life.

(6) That Free Thought is essential to progress, and that the religion of the future will be a belief in a Creed of Kinship, a charter of human and sub-human relationships.

## When Wars Will Cease

*"Let the poet cease to celebrate men's achievements in battle, and wars will cease."*
—JOAQUIN MILLER

But when will wars cease? And why, the reader may ask, if so many good reasons can be alleged against warfare, do wars still persist? I should say that they persist because, immediately, and in the first place, the militarists like them to do so, and ultimately because sentimentalists prate about them as if they were beautiful and heroic.

In saying that the military folk have a real relish for wars, I do not of course mean that, if they had their way, the country would never be free from quarrel, or that when there is a choice between war and peace they do not prefer the peace — if it is to be had on the terms they approve. I mean that, whatever they may say in any given case, they admire warfare, and believe it to be helpful to the nation's health and hardihood, and at times actually necessary. In other words, the practice of fighting is cherished and maintained by a very powerful section of the community, a class which has reason to regard its own reputation, its own interests, as closely concerned therein.

This being so, it is not surprising that such institutions as the Armistice Day service at the Cenotaph, the various absurd parades and inspections, meetings of "Old Contemptibles," and the like, are so religiously maintained. They serve a very definite purpose, and fully justify the remarks made by a socialist Member of Parliament on a recent occasion.*

> "I am thankful this mockery is over for another year. This service would have been abandoned before but for the gentlemen at the War Office, who realise that their jobs are safe while the crowd at the Cenotaph are hypnotised by the white-robed clergymen."

To such a pitch has this glorification of warfare been carried that in some quarters there is an insolent attempt to represent the policy of a simple pacifist body, such as the "No More War" Movement, as "bordering on sedition." Is it surprising, in these circumstances, that wars do not cease?

The influence of some powerful newspapers, where questions of militarism are concerned, is wholly bad; others, without openly advocating or eulogising war, indirectly promote it by the prominence they give in their columns to military subjects, as, for

*Dr. Alfred Salter, as reported, November 14th, 1932.

instance, by inviting letters which tell anecdotes of the battlefield, and what is more seductive than any other form of invitation, by offering to pay for them.

Of the same nature is the assurance, frequently given, that the British Navy is one of the chief factors that make for the peace of the world; in which confused statement an armed neutrality between powerful nations is called "peace," as if it were actually that friendly state to which pacifists aspire! This was seen, for instance, in a "message" sent on Trafalgar Day, 1932, by the president of the Navy League, to the effect that "Nelson, who disliked war as much as any pacifist of the present time, had no doubts that the Empire, as he knew it, rested, under Providence, wholly upon the national strength at sea." There followed a warning against negligence "lest the spirit of patriotism and self-sacrifice, which our greatest sea-officer bequeathed to us, be undermined by uninformed clamour."

Note the mention of Nelson's dislike of war; the pious allusion to "under Providence"; and the hint at a contrast between the "patriotism" of naval officers and the "uninformed clamour" of certain other persons! It would be comical, if such terrible consequences were not involved. How is a courageous deed performed in "the trenches" more worthy of honour than if it is done elsewhere?

It is by such indirect advocacy, by the eulogies that are never lacking for military services of any kind, that wars are maintained. It has been pointed out by Joaquin Miller that it is the supposed men of peace who are themselves responsible for the wars they deprecate, the devastation they deplore. Without any sort of ingratitude to those who have fought, and perhaps fallen, for their country, and without any lack of respect for their memory, it is full time that men should make up their minds whether it is war or peace that they desire: it is useless to expend honeyed words on peace, while all the time they are sowing the seeds of war.

Miller was quite right. It is the "men of peace" who exalt the thing they deplore. The poets in all ages have been great sinners in this respect, and not least, be it noted, those whose song is of a mild and effeminate nature, like Tennyson's. The conclusion of his poem *Maud*, in its adoption of the wicked and crazy Crimean war as bringing an end to the personal sorrows of his hero, is truly amazing:

"Yet it lightened my despair,
When I thought that a war would arise in defence of the right."

Yet one finds the truth apprehended, here and there, in old writers like Sir Walter Scott, as when he makes one of his characters say (in *Woodstock*): "An excellent man, and the best of Christians, till there is a clashing of swords, and then he starts up the complete martialist, as deaf to every pacific reasoning as if he were a game-cock."

Religion, when fighting was in prospect, has never been able to resist the strenuous weight of savagery, but in every land has shaped and adapted itself to the force of national prejudice, and has quite shamelessly blessed the banners of its counrymen under the plea of patriotism. This was seen in many cases in the South African war, when there was a frenzy of soldier-worship, and a bishop assured his flock that the clergy ought to consider what priests a nation should have, which was showing so splendid a character. The same sort of nonsense was often talked during the long European struggle; indeed, among the various religious sects the Friends alone have consistently reprobated this alliance of cross with sword.

The sum of the whole matter, frankly stated, is this — that a war which is indirectly but deliberately cultivated will come. It is useless to talk of peace, and to pray for it as we do, so long as all the sentiment that men can muster is expended on war, or on ceremonies relating to war — burials in the Abbey, sermons about patriotism, and love of king and country, royal inspection of Guards of Honour, and the like. All such fooleries can be stopped, and must be stopped, if we are serious in desiring peace; for wars will never end as long as we picture them as heroic.

A recent correspondence in a daily paper has shown that while there were some combatants in the Great War who intensely hated it, there were others to whom it was little worse than a pastime. In the words of one, "Tunneller": "The consensus of opinion was that they never *hated* the war; and that though there were often unpleasantly sticky times, for the most part life in the war had been fairly enjoyable, and had great advantages over the type of existence many have had to endure in these weak piping times of peace."*

*Morning Post*, October 26th, 1932.

Surely, then, of all blessings which mankind has power to achieve, Peace is the most ill-used — praised in the abstract by sermonisers and romanticists, but maligned and depreciated when a choice has to be made between arbitration and war. Even its advocates too often plead its cause in a humble and apologetic tone, instead of insisting, as they ought, that it is war, not peace, that should be the subject of reprobation, ridicule, and disdain.*

"But," it is said, "*this* war is justifiable." In every nation the naïve conviction prevails that though war in the abstract is to be deprecated, and though certain previous wars may possibly have lacked sufficient excuse, the particular conflict in which they are engaged is righteous, inevitable, one of pure defence — in their own words, "forced on us." Every people says and believes this faithfully, pathetically; yet even if we admit its truth in any rare instance, a modern war is none the less an offence against humanity. In bygone times when life was more savage, and international relations far less complex, war was perhaps not so criminal as it is now; for it was then possible for two or more countries to quarrel and "fight it out," like schoolboys, without inflicting any widespread or lasting injury. But now, so vast is the calamity of a war that to the world at large it hardly matters who, in childish phrase, "began it." It takes more than one to make a quarrel, and the two or more are jointly responsible for the results of their quarrel; a responsibility which becomes the heavier as the opportunities for arbitration increase.

And even if there still were cases in which a particular war was a necessity, that sheer necessity would be its one and only justification. All the other excuses, palliatives, and decorative embellishments of war in general are nonsense and nothing else. Take, for example, the not uncommon belief that war is a great natural "upheaval," with something mysterious in its origin, and beyond human control. There is nothing in the least mysterious or cataclysmic in the outbreak of modern wars. Antipathies and rivalries of nations there are, as of individuals, and if these are fostered and encouraged (as they certainly are) they will eventually burst into flame; but it is equally true that if they were wisely discountenanced they would at length subside. We do not excuse an individual who pleads his jealousy or thirst for revenge as a reason for violence, though personal passion is just as much

*As in that excellent book, *Captain Jinks, Hero*, by Ernest Crosby.

an "upheaval" as national hatred. Where a feud is nursed, a war will follow; but the feud does not justify the war.

Then there is that widespread idea, common among so-called religious persons (though it might well be called blasphemous), that wars are "sent" to rouse mankind from a selfish torpor. The effect of a war is precisely the opposite of this; for fighting concentrates men's thoughts on the attainment of a particular end, with complete disregard for those moralities which in peace cannot, at the worst, be denied some measure of consideration. What must be the result, when, in a considerable area of the world, many of the moral restrictions which have gradually been imposed on the primitive instincts of the race are suddenly withdrawn, and hosts of men are forced to take a deep draught of aboriginal savagery? It is not too much to say that if wars are "sent," it must be a very malignant power that sends them.

Wars will cease only when two conditions have been fulfilled — the first, that men shall have a genuine desire for peace; the second, that their feelings shall have been humanised in regard not to fighting only, but to the other conditions of life.

*The Creed of Kinship*

### *A Free Religion*

*"With disbelief belief increased."*—RICHARD JEFFERIES

I have said throughout that freedom of thought is not only not opposed to the creed of kinship, but is essential to it. It is significant that the word humanitarian has two chief meanings in the dictionary — the one a lover of humaneness, the other a disbeliever in the supernatural.

It is my hope that what may be called a free or rational religion, founded on kinship, and expressing itself in unselfish deeds, will eventually take the place of the many superstitious beliefs that have in the past been regarded as religions, and in many cases continue to be so honoured. From the Rev. Francis Wood's book on *Suffering and Wrong*, I would quote this excellent remark about a new religion:

"We need," he says, "a religion which shall declare men brothers not merely in a religious sense, but by reason of their essential and universal nature and needs . . . , which shall declare our present divisions and distinctions of rich and poor, master and servant, employer and employee, to be all wrong — wrong because issuing from, and tending to perpetuate the spirit of selfishness and exclusiveness."

This is itself a religion, and one which the established forms do not supply. The faith of which I write will, in my belief, be a faith not of mysteries but of verities; indeed the attempts to see everywhere the working of a divine power seem to me to do little good, while indirectly they are a hindrance to the advance of thought, by fostering a belief that, with religion inviting us, humanitarian teaching is unneeded. Why trouble, we think, concerning the welfare of mere prisoners, or animals, when matters of much higher moment are calling? The result is inevitable.

I have stated in this book my conviction that the various schools of humane thinkers, religionist or rationalist as may be, will have to find a common ground of belief before any final success can be attained. But it is evident that this is a matter for a distant age, and that at present, and for many years to come, in such protests as are made against any surviving forms of barbarity, humanitarians must dwell as little as possible on the points wherein they differ among themselves. There must be at least what might be called a truce, upon matters of religious opinion, between reformers who cling to the old faiths and those who have a newer creed of their own.

As one who has long worked for the cause of the lower animals, I have felt anxious that the zoophilist movement should be consolidated, not divided; and therefore, in such books as my *Animals' Rights* and *The Logic of Vegetarianism*, I have always refrained from criticism of the orthodox creeds, feeling that persons of all persuasions should on ethical subjects be able to work in unison.

It is the habit of religionists and of scientists alike, when referring to morality, to speak of it as something apart, something which will have to be brought into harmony and conjunction with science or religion. "One of the greatest tasks before the human race," according to General Smuts, "will be to link up science with ethical values, and thus remove the grave dangers threatening our future.'' That is most true; but might not the case be still more strongly stated? For how can any conduct which is *not* ethically just be either religious or scientific; and how can a science or a religion be worthy of the name, unless it assumes the fulfilment of all ethical duties?

The same holds true of Rationalism itself: it is void and without value unless it carries with it that sense of kinship and brotherhood which the world so grievously lacks to-day. Full freedom of thought is essential for humane progress, because otherwise the old superstitions stand in the way; but it is not of itself all that is needed, and as long as cruelty and injustice are rampant it is small consolation to be told that our religious beliefs *may* be made rational. They *must* give practical proof of their rationality. Yet to-day one may receive lists of ''libertarian'' publications, in which not one word is said on the subject of humaneness.

As far as religion is concerned — and my contention is that the future faith will be a religion — the central fact is summed up in one of Mahatma Gandhi's sayings: ''True religion is identical with morality.'' What the churches have believed in the past, or what the scientists may discover in the future, is of infinitely less moment than what the human heart shall ultimately approve as beautiful and gracious. A creed so simple may at present appear but slight and negligible, in comparison with the complicated doctrines which theology has piled up: in reality, as the one sure and abiding hope for mankind, it will include and outlast them all.

The superman is doubtless coming in the fulness of time; and his advent will best be forwarded by the patient and gradual process of fostering love and comradeship in place of hatred and self-seeking — a much larger love, and a much wider comradeship, than that of which either the religionists or the rationalists have talked. . . .

*The Creed of Kinship*

We are living in an age which still permits great wealth and abject poverty to exist side by side; we still hang and flog; we still wage wars, and honour in every way the trade of soldiering; we still ill-treat, hunt, cage, eat, and even vivisect, sentient beings closely akin to ourselves; and we still maintain a religion which does not attempt to teach us how savage these practices are. In spite of scientific discoveries and our boast of high "civilisation," many of our doings deserve rather to be classed with the primeval — the prehistoric.

Yet there is comfort in the thought that the Future is before us, and that if a hundred years effect but little change, a thousand may effect more, and ten thousand more still; there is, in fact, no limit to the time in which humane influences may be brought to bear on this brutal and barbarous mankind. . . .

*The Creed of Kinship*

Humanitarians, then, must expect little, but claim much; must know that they will see no present fruits of their labours, but that their labours are nevertheless of far-reaching importance. Let those who have been horrified by the spectacle of an atrocious war resolve to support the peace movement more strongly than ever; but let them also support the still wider and deeper humanitarian movement of which pacifism is but a part, inasmuch as all humane causes, though seemingly separate, are ultimately and essentially one.

*Seventy Years Among Savages*

### *Epitaph on a Humanitarian*

Here pause, in memory of a man
  Less careful than most are
To 'scape the fashionable ban
  On such as 'go too far'.
For him, Religion was the vow
  To work no creature's ill:
Folk groaned, 'He goes too far.' And now
He *has* gone — farther still.

*Cum Grano*

# SELECTED BIBLIOGRAPHY

*Animals' Rights Considered in Relation to Social Progress.* London: George Bell & Sons, 1892. New York: Macmillan, 1894. Various reprints in England and the United States. Final revised edition: London: George Bell and Sons, 1922. The 1892 ed. was reprinted by the Society for Animal Rights, Inc. of Clarks Summit, Pennsylvania in 1980 and published by Centaur Press in the UK. Quotations in this anthology are from the 1922 edition.

*The Call of the Wildflower.* London: Allen & Unwin, 1922.

*Company I Have Kept.* London: George Allen & Unwin, 1930.

*Consolations of a Faddist.* London: A. C. Fifield, 1906.

*The Creed of Kinship.* London: Constable & Co., 1935. New York: E. P. Dutton & Co., 1935.

*Cum Grano, Verses and Epigrams.* Berkeley Heights, New Jersey: Oriole Press, 1931.

*De Quincey.* London: George Bell and Sons, 1904. New York: Macmillan, 1904.

*Eton under Hornby: Some Reminiscences and Reflections.* London: A. C. Fifield, 1910.

*The Flogging Craze: A Statement of the Case Against Corporal Punishment.* London: George Allen & Unwin, 1916.

*A Group of Unpublished Letters by Henry S. Salt to Joseph Ishill.* Berkeley Heights, N.J.: Oriole Press, 1942.

*The Heart of Socialism.* London: Independent Labour Party, 1928.

*The Humanities of Diet, Some Reasonings and Rhymings.* London: The Humanitarian League, 1897. Manchester: The Vegetarian Society, 1914.

*Life of Henry David Thoreau.* London: Richard Bentley & Son, 1890. London: Walter Scott, Ltd., 1896.

*The Life of James Thomson ("B.V.").* London: Reeves and Turner, 1889. Reprinted several times.

*Literary Sketches.* London: Swan Sonnenschein, 1888.

*The Logic of Vegetarianism*. London: Vegetarian Jubilee Library, 1899.
*Memories of Bygone Eton*. London: Hutchinson & Co., 1928.
*On Cambrian and Cumbrian Hills*. London: A. C. Fifield, 1908. London: C. W. Daniel, 1922.
*Our Vanishing Wildflowers*. London: Watts and Co., 1928.
*Percy Bysshe Shelley: Poet and Pioneer*. London: W. Reeves, 1896. New York: Charles Scribner's Sons, 1896. London: A. C. Fifield, 1905. Several additional reprints.
*Richard Jefferies: A Study*. London: Swan Sonnenschein, 1894.
*Richard Jefferies: His Life and His Ideals*. London: A. C. Fifield, 1905.
*Seventy Years Among Savages*. London: George Allen & Unwin, 1921.
*The Song of the Respectables and Other Verses*. Manchester: Labour Press Society, 1896.
*The Story of Aeneas: Virgil's "Aeneid"*. Cambridge: Cambridge University Press, 1928.
*Tennyson As A Thinker*. London: William Reeves, 1893. Reprinted several times.
*Treasures of Lucretius: Selected Passages from the 'De Rerum Natura'*, translated by Henry S. Salt. London: Watts and Co., 1912.

## BIOGRAPHICAL AND CRITICAL STUDIES OF SALT

Hendrick, George. *Henry Salt: Humanitarian Reformer and Man of Letters*. Urbana: University of Illinois Press, 1977.
Winsten, Stephen. *Salt and His Circle*. London: Hutchinson & Co., 1951.